Eating From the Tree of Life

Daily Scripture Meditations to Ignite Your Spiritual Life

Pastor Mark Hoffman

Eating From the Tree of Life, Daily Scripture Meditations to Ignite Your Spiritual Life by Pastor Mark Hoffman

Copyright 2022 by Mark Hoffman

ISBN: 9798844050374

Unless otherwise indicated, scripture quotations are taken from the *New American Standard Bible*® (NSAB) 1960, 1962, 1963, 1968, 1971, 1972, 1973, 1975, 1995, by the Lockman Foundation. Used by permission.

For more information from Pastor Mark Hoffman, visit www.Foothillschurch.org/media/sermons

DEDICATION

To all the people of Foothills Christian Church whom I have had the privilege to grow with and pastor for 37 years, and to our wonderful staff who have served so faithfully, lovingly and skillfully, and above all to my brother and Foothills Church co-founder David, I gratefully dedicate this book. I want to especially thank my beautiful wife and life partner, Linda, who had the vision for this book and without whose encouragement, support and involvement this book would not exist.

HOW TO USE THIS BOOK

This book is the culmination of 45 years of study, teaching, ministering and following Jesus. In it I have attempted to encapsulate much of what I have learned and taught. It is not designed to be a typical "daily devotional," where you move each day to the next chapter. Rather, they are short meditations on powerful scriptural principals and truths to meditate on until you have absorbed them and incorporated them into your life. This may mean spending several days on a chapter and then later returning to it at a future date until these truths become a part of you. These Biblical truths will ignite spiritual growth and maturity in you as you put them into practice.

TABLE OF CONTENTS

God Is a Rewarder

"And without faith it is impossible to please God, because anyone who comes to Him must believe that He exists and that He rewards those who earnestly seek Him." Hebrews 11:6 (NIV)

This passage describes true Biblical faith that pleases God. True faith requires believing two things. First that God exists and second that He is a rewarder of those who earnestly seek Him. It is obvious that you can't have faith if you don't believe God exists. It's amazing anyone can doubt God's existence. He has made His existence evident. Wherever you look you see astonishing order, design and complexity. For instance, one tiny cell of DNA contains enough information to fill a library of 500 books each of 300 pages.

The majority of Americans look around at the incredible complexity of the world and say, "There must be a God - I believe He exists." This is what most people mean when they say they have faith. But this alone is not biblical faith. It is not enough to believe that God is. You must be convinced of one more thing. You must believe that He is a rewarder of those that seek Him. You must say, "God is a rewarder. If I seek Him and obey Him, He will reward me." The majority of those who say they believe God exists are not seeking Him. They don't, for instance, attend church regularly, study their Bibles, evangelize or tithe. There is only one possible reason for this. They do not believe that God is a rewarder of those who seek Him.

The two most important questions that will determine the future course of your life are: do you believe there is a God and do you believe He is a rewarder? Tomorrow you may face a difficult choice. Whether you make the difficult choice of doing the right thing will depend on whether you believe God is a rewarder. If you don't believe He is a rewarder you will stop short of full obedience when the cost seems too high. I have been able to do a number of difficult and unpopular things because I knew that God was my rewarder.

When you believe God is a rewarder you will act in order to get the promised blessing or reward. Mere belief without action is incomplete faith, it is not biblical faith. For electricity to work you must complete the circuit. Faith is like that. Without action faith is short circuited. Belief and acting must go together to complete the circuit. That is what James means when he wrote, *"faith without works is dead"* (James 2:26). It is short circuited. Faith requires actively pursuing God's promises based on conviction that God is a rewarder.

Ephesians 2:8 tells us something wonderful. It says faith is a gift of God. *Faith is the God given ability to believe God's Word and the power to act upon that belief.* Faith gives you the power to see beyond your circumstances. Faith allows you to believe in what you can't see. In fact, faith is a new way of seeing. The eye is the physical organ by which we see the physical world. Faith is the spiritual organ by which we see spiritual realities. Therefore, faith allows you to see a more complete picture of reality than other people see. One person worries when they see a stack of bills on the table which requires more money than they have. Another person with faith sees the same stack but also see a God who is faithful and bigger than problem. The second person is on the way to overcoming. Do you believe God is a rewarder? How will this affect how you live today?

Prayer - I want to have a faith that pleases You! I don't just believe that You exist, or even that You can do anything. More than that, I believe that You are faithful and are a rewarder! Help me have the courage to fully obey and act so I may receive the fullness of Your blessings and promises.

Day 2

The Rewards of Diligence

"Ask, and it will be given to you; seek, and you will find; knock, and it will be opened to you. For everyone who asks receives, and he who seeks finds, and to him who knocks it will be opened."
Matthew 7:7-8

Many have unnecessarily struggled with these verses and wonder how they can be taken literally. But when you look it at in the original Greek of the New Testament (which is a far more precise language with 6 verb tenses to English's mere 3) it reveals a powerful principle. In the Greek the words *ask, seek* and *knock* are in the present tense imperatives, giving them the literal meaning of - *ask and keep asking, seek and keep seeking and knock and keep knocking.* In giving us this promise, Jesus is underscoring the power of the Biblical Principle of "Diligence and Perseverance." "Diligence" can be defined as *a constant, steady effort to achieve* and "perseverance" as *the continuing of that effort in the face of hardship or difficulty.*

God desires to give us every good thing. He wants to give us what we are asking for, to find what we are seeking and to have the doors we are knocking on open before us. However, there are certain risks that go with freedom, promotion and prosperity. Because God loves us, He prepares us to overcome those dangers and risks by developing character and patience in us. This generally requires that the things we seek don't come quickly or easily, but that we must struggle and persevere to attain them. In this way we build the necessary muscles, as it were, for each new phase. We see this in nature. A baby chick must struggle greatly to emerge from its egg. He pecks at that egg

4

many hours gaining strength from the struggle that prepares it for the rigors of the outside world. If you help the chick out, by cracking the egg, the chick will die because it is not yet strong enough to survive. The same thing can be observed with a butterfly struggling to emerge from its cocoon.

God wants His children to grow in possessions and blessings, but even more that we grow in character. That means that character development must often precede receiving what we desire. This flies in the face of our culture's "got to have it all now" instant gratification society. People want and insist on things before they are prepared to use them in a positive and beneficial way. People want instant success and privilege. They go deep into debt so they can "have it all now." However human nature is such that riches and power gained too soon end up doing us more harm than good. Consider movie stars, rock stars and pro athletes who achieve great wealth and fame quickly. They are often destroyed by it because they are not prepared. Developing diligence and perseverance are an indispensable part of our being good and successful stewards of God's riches.

God has so constructed the world that it surrenders its blessings and secrets to those who understand the principle of diligence and perseverance, *"The plans of the diligent lead surely to abundance, but everyone who is hasty comes only to poverty"* (Prov. 21:5). If you have a plan that is pleasing to God, and you add diligence and perseverance to it, you will surely move toward abundance and success. Likewise, diligence allows you to advance, be promoted and gain influence, *"The hand of the diligent will rule, but the slack hand will be put to forced labor"* (Prov. 12:24). People who receive great advantages and opportunities and yet lack diligence and perseverance can seldom capitalize on their good fortunes (Prov. 12:27).

Diligence not only gains us God's blessings but, more importantly, it deepens our relationship with God because, "*He is a rewarder of them that diligently seek Him*" (Heb. 11:6 KJV). In order to diligently seek Him we must set aside regular times of fellowship, prayer and Bible reading. Diligence means that we remain faithful to church fellowship and devotions and do not alter our spiritual commitments every time it involves some inconvenience, or our schedule changes.

Great harvests do not come from flashfloods or sudden torrential rains. Just as bountiful crops are the result of regular, gentle rains so blessings and spiritual growth come as a result of consistent, faithful obedience. Many people, after a camp or conference, or some other experience with God, engage in a short season of great activity, and then burn out and drop out before seeing their hopes realized. A part of diligence is holding onto the things God has shown us or given us by putting them into practice until they bring their blessing and increase. If we are careless with them, then we can let the harvest slip away from us. Remember, diligence means that you keep asking, seeking and knocking until our faithful God rewards you. If you do this, the blessing of this world and the riches of His kingdom will be given to you.

Prayer- Thank You for Your great generosity. Teach me to be a diligent, fruitful and faithful steward. Help me value the spiritual blessings over the earthly ones and to diligently pursue them. Strengthen me to keep asking, keep seeking and keep knocking, encouraged by the knowledge that You are faithful.

Walk With the Spirit

"I will ask the Father, and He will give you another Helper, that He might be with you forever; that is the Spirit of truth, whom the world cannot receive, because it does not see Him or know Him, but you know Him because He abides with you and will be in you." John 14:16

On the last night Jesus was with His disciples He told them He was leaving them. But then He comforted them with the above words. Jesus had been their Helper and Guide but now *another* Helper and Guide, similar to the first, would be sent them. The same Spirit who had abided with them in the person of Jesus would soon be in them. The Greek word translated as "Helper" is the word *Paraclete* which means *"along-side of."* Just as Jesus had walked alongside them, so now the Holy Spirit would walk alongside them. In the same way the Holy Spirit is given to walk alongside us. May I ask you, what is your relationship with the Holy Spirit like? You may have never thought in those terms before. But remember that the Holy Spirit is not a force or power but a person. He is the third person of the Trinity. The disciples had a relationship with Jesus. They talked, laughed and went through difficulties and victories together. Jesus promised that the new Helper would be similar. He would be a companion and friend.

The Holy Spirit is our Helper and Guide who is alongside us through every challenge, ready to guide, strengthen and comfort us. To truly follow Jesus, we must go through life joined to a power and love greater than our own. After His resurrection Jesus told His disciples to wait in Jerusalem until they received the Baptism of the Holy Spirit (Acts 1:4-5). Even though He had taught and trained them for 3 years they were not yet prepared. It is the same for you and me. You can come from a great Christian family, know the Bible backwards and forwards, have a degree from a Christian university, and belong to a great church, but it is not enough. Like the disciples, we need the Baptism of the Holy Spirit.

God's plan is not only that we are born again by the Spirit, but that from that moment on we learn to draw guidance and strength from the Spirit. The Apostle Paul wrote, *"If we live by the Spirit, let us also walk by the Spirit"* (Gal. 5:25). To *"walk by the Spirit"* means that our daily manner of life is led and empowered by the Holy Spirit. We should look to Him as we face each new circumstance and opportunity. Cheerful obedience to God's Spirit is the highest form of obedience. It is by daily yielding our mind and emotions to the Holy Spirit that we become transformed into Christ's image.

When we were first planting our church many years ago, someone introduced us to a helpful concept they referred to as "leaning into the anointing of the Spirit." We were young when we began our church and had only been youth pastors before. There were many things we were called on to do for the very first time such as comfort the dying, marriage counseling, casting out demons, doing funerals and much more. Often we felt unprepared. But we were told that since God had called and anointed us to be pastors, we could just "lean into the anointing" and we would find that the Holy Spirit would equip us in the moment and make us fully adequate. This is of course not only true for pastors but for every Christian. In any situation, no matter how overwhelming it is, you can count on the anointing of the Spirit to enable you. Wherever God leads you, and into whatever situation you are thrust, the Holy Spirit will enable you. Jesus told His apostles, who were fisherman and common folk, that they would be brought before rulers or authorities, but that they should not worry or feel inadequate, *"for the Holy Spirit will teach you in that very hour what you ought to say"* (Luke 12:12). The Bible teaches us that we should prepare ourselves and make plans, but we should never be afraid of being in situations we feel unprepared for because we can rely on the anointing of the Holy Spirit.

Spiritual maturity comes from walking in the Spirit. It comes from making those small adjustments of attitude and attention that allow us to be led and strengthened by Him throughout the day. That's why it begins by our becoming more aware of His presence, *"For those who are according to the flesh set their minds on the things of the flesh, but those who are according to the Spirit, the things of the Spirit"* (Rom. 8:5).

Let me ask again, what is your relationship with the Holy Spirit like? Is He a continual reality to you? Do you go through each day with Him? Do you consider Him in your speech and actions? Remember, He is a person and the Bible teaches us that we can cause Him grief (Eph. 4:30), and we can quench or dampen His activity in us (I Thess. 5:19). Do you honor and acknowledge the Holy Spirit in your life. Do you silently talk to Him as you go through the day? Do you say, "Please lead me as I go into this meeting," "Please give me Your love for this difficult person I am going to see," "Give me your wisdom as I face this decision?" Do you thank Him for His Help and praise Him throughout the day? If you do, the Holy Spirit will be your great Helper.

Prayer - Thank You for being my Guide, Helper, Companion and Friend. Help me to become more aware of You in my Life. Please teach me to trust in Your enabling power and wisdom in each situation. I honor and worship You, my wonderful Holy Spirit.

Triumphing Over Fear

"There is no fear in love; but perfect love casts out fear…. the one who fears is not perfected in love." I John 4:18

If you do a concordance search you will discover that the Bible contains over 600 occurrences of the words *fear, fearful, afraid* and *anxious*. Fear is a constant reality for humans. Learning to overcome fear is a necessary part of life. This is true even for God's people. The words *"fear not", "don't be afraid",* and *"take courage"* were spoken over 300 times to believers.

Our opening verse teaches us something very important about fear. Before we can ever fear we must first doubt God's love, because *"There is no fear in love; but perfect love drives out fear"* (NIV). This means that if you struggle with fears and anxieties, your real problem is a love problem – you do not fully know God's love. Therefore, the way to overcome fear is to come into a greater experience of God's love for you. When you try to fight your fears and anxieties directly, you focus on them, and give them an even bigger place in your mind. But when you focus on God's love, then His perfect love drives fear from your heart and mind. As we grow secure in our Father's love and care, our fears fade away.

God puts within each of our hearts a deep and life-transforming revelation that He is our Father and we are His children. Paul writes, *"Because you are sons, God has sent forth the Spirit of His Son into our hearts, crying, 'Abba, Father!'"* (Gal. 4:6). Jesus' own

Spirit brings a powerful conviction to our hearts that we are indeed God's children. In the very next verse, Paul brings forward a powerful truth. He continues, *"Therefore you are no longer a slave, but a son; and if a son, then an heir though God"* (Gal. 4:7). Think about what this means. Slaves serve out of fear. They know that they can be sold or cast away if at any time they displease their master or don't perform satisfactorily. But sons and daughters serve out of love because they know they belong and are held securely in love. They know they are rightful heirs to every good thing.

Almost everything people do they do either to GAIN love, or because they ARE loved. When we labor to try to get people to love us, we are slaves. We live in fear of not being loved and of not having enough. But when we joyfully serve because we are loved and are heirs, then we truly live as sons and daughters. Satan wants to separate us from experiencing God's love. He seeks to inject fear into our hearts so that we take our eyes off of God's love. If he can make us afraid, he can pressure us into bad choices and compromises, so that we lose our freedom. Remember, the devil seeks to drive us with fear and weaken us with despair. But God always leads us with peace and strengthens us with joy.

Remember when the disciples were in a boat far from land in the midst of a terrible storm? The waves were breaking over the boat, and Jesus was asleep in the stern. The disciples were greatly afraid. They woke Jesus up and He stilled the storm. Do you remember what He said to them next?

He said, *"Why are you afraid? Do you still have no faith?"* (Mark 4:40). Their fear revealed their lack of faith. If you have a fear problem, it means you also have a faith problem, for fear and faith are opposites. One drives out the other. Fear incapacitates us and makes us unproductive. It therefore robs us of many blessings. Faith, on the other hand, both ignites us and steadies us at the same time.

Complete obedience depends upon total trust that God is in control. All fear for the Christian is rooted in a lack of trust in God's love and faithfulness to us. Fear makes us draw back from full obedience. If you look far enough into the disobedience of any Christian, you will find fear – fear of not having enough, of not being enough, and of not being loved or cared for. Do not let the devil or the world sow fear into your heart. The antidote to fear is simple, childlike faith. Jesus said, *"Do not let your heart be troubled; believe in God, believe also in Me"* (John 14:1).

Prayer – Forgive me for the times I have chosen to fear rather than rest in Your love. I choose to live as a son rather than as a slave. Help me to trust You totally so I can obey You completely.

Jesus the Servant

"For who is greater, the one who is at the table or the one who serves? Is it not the one who is at the table? But I am among you as one who serves." Luke 22:27

Although Jesus was the King of Kings, He expressed that authority by serving. He also bore the awesome glory of His Father, yet He demonstrated that glory through ministering to others. He said, *"I am among you as one who serves."* Jesus defined Himself by service. He said that He did not come to be served, but to serve (Matt. 20:28). He redefined greatness. The greatest people I have known have all learned the joy and blessing of serving.

Jesus said that He came that we might have life in all its abundance (John 10:10). Jesus came not only to bring us forgiveness by dying on the cross for us, He also came to teach us how to live the abundant life. Living the abundant life requires more than just accepting Jesus' sacrifice for us. It also calls for following Jesus' teaching and example. Jesus was the greatest servant who ever lived. Many people selfishly pursue happiness but it eludes them, or if they temporality find it, it doesn't last. But when you serve others, you are blessed and you enjoy the abundant life. The people I know that have the greatest joy all have one thing in common - they serve others. *They have learned that you make a living by what you earn but you make a life by what you give.*

We will never know the abundant life until we begin to serve. From the age of 17 through 23 I lived only for myself. My every decision was based upon what I thought would make me the happiest. The result was that I became fairly miserable. At age 23 I began to follow Jesus and serve others. I found the life that only Jesus could give me. *If you want the life that only God can give you, you must be willing to lay down the life you have and serve others for Jesus' sake.* Serving others doesn't come natural to most of us. We make the excuse that we have problems of our own to deal with or that others don't deserve our help.

Consider the last night of Jesus' life. He knew that the hour of His suffering had come (John 13:1). He knew that in just a few hours He would be arrested, falsely accused, beaten, mocked and crucified. He also knew that his disciples would abandon Him and that Peter would deny Him three times. He had a lot on His mind. And then it happened. He noticed that no one had washed the disciples' feet, as was customary. Perhaps He waited a few moments to see if any of them would do it. But no one moved. So Jesus got up, took off His nice outer garments and washed their feet. It was more than an act of kindness; it was an expression of who He was. He said it was also an expression of who we should be (John 13:13-14).

The secret to becoming like Jesus is to go beyond *just believing* the right things and *beginning to do* what Jesus did. When we do this, relying on the power of the Spirit, we will find our life transformed. Do you want to know Jesus and have deep fellowship with Him? Remember, Jesus walks among us, but He is here as One who serves. When we begin to serve others, our eyes are opened and we find fellowship with Jesus everywhere. We serve others for Jesus' sake (Matt. 10:39). This means that our motive in serving is to please Jesus, and our reward is to know His pleasure with us regardless of how others respond. Partner with Jesus today by serving others.

Prayer - Help me to follow You in serving others. I want to discover the fellowship I can have with You as I serve others for Your sake. Help me to be content in serving others knowing I am pleasing You, despite how others may respond.

How to Walk by Faith

"Now the LORD said to Abram,
'Go forth from your country, and from your relatives
and from your father's house, to the land which I will show you;
and I will make you a great nation, and I will bless you,
and make your name great; and so you shall be a blessing.'"
Genesis 12:1-2

Abraham lived among His idol-worshiping relatives in Chaldea (modern day Iraq). One day God called to Abraham and said, "I have something more for you. I have a better future for you, but you will have to leave where you are and go to an unfamiliar place." God had to bring Abraham out of the safe and comfortable place he knew in order to bring him to a better place. God's promises couldn't come to pass where he was. We all like to be brought into something better. What we don't like is having to leave or be pushed out of where we feel comfortable and safe. But sometimes that is the requirement if we are to receive from God.

The Bible says that Abraham trusted God and obeyed God's call. *"By faith Abraham, when he was called, obeyed by going out to a place which he was to receive for an inheritance; and he went out, not knowing where he was going"* (Heb. 11:8). The place was Canaan, a place completely foreign and unfamiliar to Abraham. Faith requires leaving the familiar and journeying into the unknown. That journey can seem risky and leave you feeling vulnerable. It must have seemed overwhelming to Abraham, but we read that Abraham obeyed by faith. Faith allows us to accomplish great things and lay hold of great promises. But faith comes at a cost. You must be willing to surrender your illusion of control over your life and instead face the unknown future, trusting only in God.

Hebrews 11 opens up with one of the clearest definitions of faith in the Bible. *"Now faith is the substance of things hoped for, the evidence of things not seen"* (Heb. 11:1 NKJV). It says that faith is an *evidence* that is beyond any of your physical senses. It has *substance*, although you can't hold it in your hand. Faith is not believing without evidence. But it requires understanding that the evidence has been put inside you by God. It is a supernatural evidence. Some translations use words like "assurance" or "conviction," but I believe the King James best translates the Greek words, *hupostasis* and *elegos*. Faith is the God-given tangible proof inside us that what we believe is real. Faith doesn't deny reality. It allows you to see more of reality than unbelievers can see. The eye allows you to only see the physical world, but God-given faith allows you to "see" spiritual realities. For instance, love is not visible to the physical eye, but life is not worth living without it. God isn't visible, but He is the most important reality of all.

II Corinthians 5:7 says, *"for we walk by faith, not by sight."* Faith is a new way to navigate through life. It is a skill we grow in. Walking by faith begins with a commitment to discipline myself to not react to circumstances but rather to respond by faith. We were created to live by faith – it's how God made us. People try to live without faith, but they lack the power, wisdom and love to live well. Without faith, people become soul sick. They stagger through life and get lost.

God's calling you to follow Him out to an unfamiliar place. You must walk by faith to get there. God is waiting to meet you there. You must be willing to leave your comfort zone – I call it your "*containment zone*" because you may feel comfortable there, but you can't grow beyond its limits. Do you believe God has something better for you? Are you willing to go to a land you don't know? Will you say to God, "I am willing to follow You into the unknown – because that's where my promised land lies?"

Prayer – I want to leave the familiar and journey with You into an unknown better future. I will surrender the mere illusion that I can control life. I will trust You to lead and guide me. I will trust in Your provision. Help me to grow in my ability to walk by faith rather than sight.

It's Important to Remember

"Only be careful, and watch yourselves closely so that you do not forget the things your eyes have seen or let them fade from your heart as long as you live. Teach them to your children and to their children after them." Deuteronomy 4:9 (NIV)

At the end of Moses' life, he recounts to Israel God's faithfulness over the past 40 years. In the speech he includes the above warning, *"do not forget the things your eyes have seen."* Imagine what their eyes had seen: the 10 plagues on the Egyptians, the Red Sea parted and Pharaoh's army destroyed, a pillar of fire and smoke which led them, water from a rock and manna from the sky. Who could ever forget that? But Israel did forget and as a result fell into bondage several times in their history. Throughout Israel's history every generation could recite the stories of the events of the exodus from Egypt and the miracles in the wilderness. How can you remember all the stories and still have it be said that you forgot? What did Moses mean by *"forgetting?"*

When we use the word "forget" we generally mean that we can't recall something to mind. We say, "I can't remember their name" or "'I can't remember where I left my keys." But in the Bible, to forget means that something has lost its power or influence over you; that some person or event that once made a great impression on you has lost its hold and effect, and is no longer important to you. You can "forget" anything. You can forget the example, words and influence of parents, teachers and mentors. You can forget how bad it felt to be lost, the joy of salvation, God's wonderful works in your life or how fulfilling ministry was. When they no longer inspire and influence you, then you have "forgotten." The devil and the world want to make us "forget." The Methodist Church has "forgotten" John Wesley. They still have his name on monuments, colleges and churches but they no longer follow his teachings or example. The devil doesn't care if we remember names and dates – as long as the power and reality of them has faded away.

Our life is determined by what we *choose* to "remember" and what we *come* to forget. Remembering is always a choice but forgetting comes naturally. We forget unless we choose to "remember." This truth came to me over 20 years ago at an evening meeting of our high school winter camp. I was watching students in tears, broken before the Lord, confessing various sins and getting "right" with God. I thought, I have seen this scene so many times with many of these same kids. I asked the Lord, "Why do people become so spiritually dull and even backslidden when they go home from camp, only to return here later and repeat the cycle?" I felt His answer come to my heart, "When they return to their secular school, non-Christian friends, busy sports schedule and worldly entertainments, they forget Me – how My love felt, how near I am to them, and the joy of salvation. And now in this place, they 'remembered.'" Most backsliding comes from forgetting, and repentance comes when you remember the goodness of God and how precious His love is. Many Christians go through these spiritual cycles of ups and downs, of forgetting and then remembering. When you remember, you advance, but it's so easy to forget.

Why do we so often forget the Lord in our lives? Several chapters later Moses gives us one answer. In chapter 6 he tells the Israelites that God will give them splendid cities that they did not build, wells that they did not dig, orchards and houses in the land He was giving them. Then he warns, *"then watch yourself, that you do not forget the Lord who brought you from the land of Egypt, out of the house of slavery"* (Deut. 6:12). Blessings can cause us to forget God. As God's gifts begin to replace sin's sorrows and hardships, we can forget how grateful we felt to Jesus when He delivered us. We can begin to focus more on the gifts than the Giver of those gifts. This passage reminds us that when we are most blessed, we can be in the most danger of forgetting God. This is one reason God allows us to go through suffering, so that we will remember our need for Him.

Of course some things need to be forgotten. *"Joseph named his firstborn son Manasseh, 'For' he said, 'God has made me forget all my trouble'"* (Gen. 41:51). Manasseh means *"causes to forget."* Joseph let God's deliverance and blessings overshadow all the terrible things others had done to him. We all have things we need to forget, so that we no longer live under their negative power and influence. We must stop brooding over and meditating on the hurtful things done to us, and focus instead on God's goodness and blessings. If we do, the damage and hurt of those things will fade away. But, if instead, we forget to count our blessings and practice thankfulness, we will remember all our hurts and fall into negativity, fear, and defeat. But when we remember the Lord's great acts on our behalf, we become confident and courageous.

Moses encouraged those on the brink of the Promised Land, with its mighty nations and armies, not to allow fear to stop them, *"you shall not be afraid of them; you shall well remember what the Lord your God did to Pharaoh and to all Egypt"* (Deut. 7:18).

Life is determined by what we choose to remember and what we allow ourselves to forget. What are you doing to help yourself "remember?" You can help yourself remember by sharing your testimony in witnessing to others, being active in worship and fellowship, thanking God regularly for your blessings, and doing daily devotions.

Prayer – Help me to remember all Your kind acts on my behalf and to thank You for my many blessings. I choose to forgive those who mistreated me, forget the wrongs I suffered, let the pain fade away, and live a life of joy and gratitude.

Speak Life

"Now if we put the bits into the horses' mouths so that they will obey us, we direct their entire body as well. Look at the ships also, though they are so great and are driven by strong winds, are still directed by a very small rudder wherever the inclination of the pilot desires. So also the tongue is a small part of the body, and yet it boasts of great things. See how great a forest is set aflame by such a small fire!" James 3:3-5

Some things are small but powerful. Ants can carry up to 50 times their weight. One species of the Box Jellyfish has enough venom to kill 20 adults. So it is with the tongue. The tongue is a small part of the body; certainly, there are far larger and more impressive parts. But is there any more powerful? Pound for pound it is the strongest muscle in the human body. Like a bridle directs a horse and a rudder determines the direction of a ship, so, for better or worse, the words we speak tend to determine the course of our lives.

One of the things that separates us from animals is our ability to use language. It's part of what it means that we are made in God's image. God created the world by speaking words, "Let there be light" and there was light (Gen. 1:3). As His final act He created a being that could also speak. Speech is a powerful thing. If you want a blessed life of loving and being loved, then you can't ignore the tongue, *"For the one who desires life, to love and see good days, must keep his tongue from evil and his lips from speaking deceit"* (I Peter 3:10). Often people look at their life full of broken relationships and shattered dreams. The look around for answers to what went wrong. Often, they look for someone to blame. But so often the answer is right under their nose - it's their tongue. A good life requires that we pay attention to our words. We dare not be careless or cruel in our words and expect happiness.

Proverbs 10:11 says, *"Death and life are in the power of the tongue and those who love it will eat its fruit."* Our words largely determine the menu or diet of our life. A person who foolishly gives their tongue free reign can destroy their own life. Even more importantly we learn that both death and life are in the tongue. I can speak words that tear people down or words that build people up. Many years ago, I had a very dear friend to whom I spoke cutting words in hurt and anger. I ruined that friendship in just a few moments. For many years I tried to restore that friendship but my friend remained cold and aloof. Only now, nearly 40 years later, is that friendship being restored. But life is also in the power of the tongue. That means that in any situation I can speak life. Words are powerful and they matter. That is why Jesus we will be held accountable for the words we speak (Matt. 12: 36).

John Maxwell says that every one of us carries around two buckets, one with gasoline and one with water. Every time we encounter a little fire of criticism, misunderstanding or gossip, we can either throw gasoline on it or we can throw water on it to diminish it. God calls us to be peace makers. Don't be one who passes on gossip or criticism. Remember, the one who slanders or passes on gossip hurts three people. First, he poisons his own soul and robs himself of God's blessings. Second, he steals a person's good name and reputation, and lastly, he hurts and defiles anyone who listen to them and ingests the poison.

Proverbs 10:11 says, "The mouth of the righteous is a fountain of life." By your words you can turn people from destruction to the path of life and wisdom. As you speak words of blessing and encouragement you breathe life into people. Don't ever underestimate your ability to build up and influence people for good with your words. My mother had the ability to always see the good in others and use her words to bring life. Every life enters our world with promise. Satan is the voice saying "no" to that promise. Jesus is the voice saying "yes" to that promise. Satan seeks people who will speak his words of cursing and destruction over people to snuff out the promise. Jesus calls us to see the promise in each life and join Him in calling it forth with words of blessing. God is at work in every person. Why not focus on where He is at work to bring growth and use our words to assist Him. I have a friend who started a school with very few resources or money. As a result, she began with many untrained and imperfect teachers. But she always found what was good in each of them and praised them for it. Every teacher got better and grew as a person. Bless what is positive in a person and help it to grow!

Your tongue is powerful! It can proclaim the good news of the Gospel and bring people to Christ. Your words can strengthen and breathe life into others. Why diminish and dishonor your tongue by using it to gossip, criticize or make course jokes. Let your words glorify Christ.

Prayer - Thank You for the wonderful gift of speech. Help me to respect and rightly use this powerful gift. I determine today to try to only use my words to build up and give life and not to tear down and destroy. Help my mouth to be a fountain of life. May my lips always be ready to share Your gospel.

Day 9

Give Thanks!

"Shout joyfully to the Lord, all the earth. Serve the Lord with gladness; come before Him with singing…. Enter His gates with Thanksgiving and His courts with praise." Psalm 100:1-2, 4

This verse tells us that if we want to come into the Lord' presence we are do it with joy, thanksgiving and praise. The ancient Israelites were to enter through the Temple gates and into its courts with thanksgiving and praise. Imagine a king ruling over his kingdom from his walled city. In order to gain an audience with the king, you would have to get past the gates of the city and then gain access to the courts of his palace. In the same way, no one can storm our Heavenly King's dwelling place and demand an audience. People may shout at the heavens and even shake their fist, but all that comes back is silence. But here we learn that an attitude of thankfulness and a heart full of praise brings us into the very court of our King. In fact, the Bible reveals that God's throne room is a place of continual thanksgiving, worship and praise (Rev. 4:8-11), and that He dwells among those who praise Him (Ps. 22:3). Thanksgiving and praise bring us into the Lord's presence.

People who live in a state of thankfulness are candidates for God's blessings because they are living out God's will for them, *"Rejoice always; pray without ceasing; in everything give thanks; for this is God's will for you in Christ Jesus"* (I Thess. 5:16-18). As we move toward God with an attitude of thanksgiving and praise, He moves toward us with

His glorious presence and help. This means that we can experience the Lord's strength and joy even in the most trying circumstances. As we begin to thank and praise the Lord, we will find ourselves being lifted out of our weakness and into His strength and comfort. One of the greatest spiritual secrets that I ever learned is taking "praise breaks" every day. Right now, stop and thank God for 10 things. If you do, you will experience the Lord's presence lifting you up and encouraging you. If you do it several times each day, your attitude and your life will change.

Thankfulness does not come natural to us. We must work at it. In Luke 11 Jesus healed ten lepers, yet only two returned to thank Him. We don't have to teach our children to say "mine" or "I want…" but we do have to teach them to say "thank you." Unfortunately, most people allow their minds to be dominated with negative thoughts. *We spend 90% of our time worrying about the 10% we don't have and only 10% being grateful for the 90% we do have.* Our attitude is the most important and decisive factor in our life. Why not develop thankfulness? Benjamin Franklin said that one sentence above all impacted his life: *"Some people grumble because God place thorns among the roses; why not thank God because He placed roses among the thorns?"* That one sentence reflects a small change in perspective that will revolutionize anyone's life. When we focus on problems instead of blessings, we feel helpless and overwhelmed, and see ourselves as victims. Our future will largely be determined by the attitudes and perspectives we choose to adopt. Why not focus on things to thank God for?

A thankful attitude helps us to maintain right thinking. It protects us from discouragement and despair. Without thankfulness we can fall into deception (Rom. 1:21). Thanksgiving and praise is like turning your satellite dish towards God so you get a better signal. It puts us on God's wavelength so we can hear Him. Think of God being on the FM frequency. When we worry, grumble and complain, we are switched into the lower AM frequency but when we are grateful and practice thankfulness, we switch to the higher FM frequency.

Developing an attitude of thankfulness can lift us above anxiety and into God's peace, *"Be anxious for nothing, but in everything by prayer and supplication WITH THANKSGIVING let your requests be made known to God. And the peace of God, which surpasses all comprehension, will guard your hearts and your minds in Christ Jesus"* (Phil. 4:6-7). There is a perfect peace available that can guard our hearts when our requests to God are linked with giving thanks to Him. Many Christians fail to enter into this peace because their prayers are little more than an expression of fear, anxiety and desperation, rather than confident faith. Before you can truly roll your concerns onto the Lord, you must enter into His presence with thanksgiving and praise. Thanking God for what He has already done for you will ignite your faith for what we are now asking. In fact, thankfulness will lift us above spiritual dullness and doubt, *"Devote yourself to prayer, keeping alert in it with an attitude of thanksgiving"* (Col. 4:2).

We can be overcomers by choosing a thankful attitude. Rather than complaining about a sink full of dirty dishes, you can choose to thank God that you have food and a family to prepare it for. If you have a blowout on the freeway, you can thank God for keeping you from injury and that you have a car and a spare tire in your trunk. In every situation you can give thanks, and if you do, you will be blessed and you will be an overcomer.

Prayer - Thank You for all Your goodness to me. I want to continually live in Your presence with joy, thanksgiving and praise. I choose to have a thankful attitude. Now from your heart thank Him for 10 or more things.

The Greatest Possession

"For though the Lord is exalted, yet He regards the lowly,
but the haughty He knows from afar."
Psalm 138:6

"God is opposed to the proud, but gives grace to the humble."
James 4:2

What do you think is the greatest possession on earth? It's greater than wealth, health, career or even finding true love. To have great intelligence, beauty, talent, and athletic ability, you must be born with it. But this possession is greater and it is available to everyone. It's the single greatest key to life. What is it? It is humility and it will enrich your life more than any other thing. It attracts God's attention and His favor. It is the opposite of pride. Pride is one of the costliest and most destructive things one can carry through life. The above passage in James tells us that God actively opposes the proud. Therefore the proud have an uphill walk into a stiff headwind as they go through life. Pride puts us on the wrong side of God. Pride is the inclination to look at yourself (and look *to* yourself) rather than the One who made you. A prideful person is full of himself which keeps him from receiving God's grace because God can't pour into something that is already full. Pride makes us boast in our strengths, despair in our weakness and wallow in guilt and shame because pride is focused on us rather than God and His grace.

Humility is different from pride. Humility means being focused outside of myself. Therefore I can recognize and defer to someone greater, stronger and wiser than I. I can therefore gain from God's wisdom and find protection in His strength. Why get stuck in your own thoughts, worries and calculations when we have available to us the greatest Mind in the universe? Why depend upon your own strength when God shares His with us? Humility is the path to life and salvation. Our walk with Jesus begins when we humble ourselves and admit we are sinners who are in need of a Savior and forgiveness. As we go forward, it remains the key to our spiritual growth. The humbler we can remain, the more we benefit from the work of the Holy Spirit in our life. The difference between pride and humility is who you place at the center of your life. When we are humble, we can be a peacemaker because we don't need to defend ourselves, for the Lord is our defense (Ps. 118:14 NIV). We can rejoice in others success because we aren't threatened by them, for we know who we are in Christ. And we never need to wallow in despair because we have the riches of God on our side.

The self-esteem message, which is so popular today, is the exact opposite of the Gospel message. It teaches us to turn inward and put our focus on and trust in ourselves. The Bible calls that pride. The Gospel teaches us to humble ourselves and put our focus and trust in God in all things. Only then can we receive from His riches. Most people don't realize that low self-esteem is as much a manifestation of pride as boastfulness. Both reflect a preoccupation with ourselves; one merely focuses on our strengths and the other on our negatives. That is why we can't escape low self-esteem unless we repent of our pride and self-absorption and put our focus on God, where it belongs. When we esteem Him and rest in His wisdom, love and promises, we find great peace and confidence. Then can we say with Paul, *"I can do all things through Him who strengthens me"* (Phil. 4:13).

Insecurity is not the opposite of pride; they are two sides of the same coin. In fact, pride inevitably produces insecurity because when we turn inward, we become focused not only on what we have, but also on what we lack and can't control. But when you are focused on the Lord, you are secure and confident in all circumstances because you trust in His faithfulness. Humility does not mean having a low opinion of yourself or your gifts. Humility is not thinking less of yourself, it is thinking of yourself less. It is turning your gaze from inward to upward. Jesus walked a humble path and we are to walk in His footsteps. Jesus overcame through humility and so can we. In Matthew chapter 5, Jesus repeats a promise to us from the Psalms, *"But the humble will inherit the land and will delight themselves in abundant prosperity"* (Ps. 37:11). Unfortunately, pride comes to us naturally but humility must be sought after and developed. Humility truly is a great possession.

Prayer - Lord, I humble myself before You and raise my gaze to up You. You are the Source of every good thing. I don't want to be full of myself but rather full of You. I want to exchange my strength for Your strength and my plans for Your plans. I want to reflect Your glory rather than seek for my own. I want to serve others as Jesus did. I want to receive the grace You pour out upon the humble.

Gaining Vision

"Where there is no vision, the people perish." Proverbs 29:18

Do you have vision for your life? The above verse tells us that it is essential for us. People without it "perish." The Hebrew word translated as "perish" is the word "para" which has the following meanings, "to let loose, let go, decline, come apart." Where there is no vision, people let themselves go, slide downward and decline. A lack of vision leads to apathy, aimlessness, a sense of helplessness and despair. A lack of vision will destroy a culture.

What is vision and why is it essential to life? The Hebrew word translated as vision is "chazon," from the root "chaza" which means "to split or divide." Vision is the sight God gives us when He "splits or divides" the surface circumstances and allows us to peer beyond them into the deeper realities. Vision is an inspired view of God's purposes in the circumstances around you and the role He wants you to play in them. Vision allows you to see with God's perspective. God sees things far differently than we do. God is never overwhelmed, confused, defeated or out of answers. Many people feel helpless and complain about the present circumstances.

Vision allows you to not just see things as they are, but as God wants to make them. God wants to give us vision for our family, career, church and society.

God created us to partner with Him in bringing about His plans and purposes. That's why people don't live well without vision; it's a violation of our human nature and a denial of our human spirit. This is why people say, "There must be more to life." It's why many people go through mid-life crisis because they realize they have lived without vision. Helen Keller, who was blind and deaf, was once asked if there was anything worse than being blind. "Yes," she answered, "to be able to see but have no vision." Without vision people grow anxious, petty and selfish. People increasingly just go through the motions and channel surf through life. Right now, people are taking drugs, pulling levers on slot machines and playing online games for hours because they haven't heard from God. One word from God would ignite them and set them on a positive new course, "He sent His Word and healed them and delivered them from all their destructions" (Ps. 107:20). This is exactly what happened to me at age 23. A person's life changes when they receive vision from God and realize that God wants to use them to help change the world. We must carry His vision for our society if we are to be its salt and light.

Can every Christian receive vision for their life? The answer is yes. With the outpouring of the Holy Spirit, the Apostle Peter announced that now all people could hear from God and have visions and dreams (Acts 2:16-17). Being led by the Spirit should mark every believer's life (Rom. 8:14). So how do we gain vision? Gaining vision begins by knowing and following God's Word. In the OT God gave us His mandate to multiply, fill the earth, subdue it and steward it for Him (Gen. 1:28). In the NT we are told to teach and make disciples of Jesus among all peoples (Matt. 28:18-20). God gives us unique gifts, talents and vision so we can accomplish our part in His great enterprise. The Bible is the map that helps get you to the place where you are ready to hear Him. It will teach you the ways of God and prepare you to hear and recognize what He says. As we walk in God's general will, we become candidates for God to speak specific vision to us, "For to him who has, more will be given" (Matt. 13:12).

Next, consecrate your imagination to God. Jesus taught that

growth and change take place at the level of our imagination. Therefore, we must take care what we allow to fill our imagination, "Take care what you listen to. By your standard of measure it will be measured to you" (Mark 4:24). The words and images we listen to begin to form an inner lens in our imagination by which we measure, interpret and form our expectations of life. Since God's vision is formed in our imagination, we must dedicate the imaginations of our heart to Him. Filling our imaginations with worldly dreams and amusements leads to aimlessness and defeat. God wants to paint His visions in our imagination as we meditate upon His Word and His great deeds. The Prophet Asaph found himself in a very difficult situation and wrote, "I will remember Your wonders of old. I will ponder all Your work and meditate on your mighty deeds" (Ps. 77:11-12). Asaph knew that if he would fill his imagination with God's past mighty works, then God would fill his imagination with vision on how to overcome what he was facing.

Finally, we must be diligent and patient. Vision often comes gradually, as a growing conviction in us, that God wants us to do something. The vison develops over time and can't be rushed. We must be like a bird with its egg and incubate the vision until it is fully developed. We must be willing to serve another people's vision. When we do, it helps our own vision develop and be clarified. Our influence for good will rise no higher than our vision. Vision will partner you with the creative power of God. Remember, great victories or great defeats begin in the imaginations of our heart.

Prayer- I want to see with Your perspective. I want to see everything the way You want to make it. I want You to use me and make me a part of Your plan. Give me vision for my life, family, church and city.

A Renewed Mind

"And do not be conformed to this world, but be transformed by the renewing of your mind, so that you may prove what the will of God is, that which is good and acceptable and perfect."
Romans 12:2

We generally find life to be about what we expect. We interpret things to conform to our thoughts and expectations. We live out what we believe to be true. While some blame others or bad luck for how their life turned out, the truth is, most of our problems stem from our own thinking and choices. So, if you want to see your life change, you must begin with your thinking.

The above verse contrasts being conformed to being transformed. To be conformed means that outer pressures have pressed you into shape. You live in reaction to social pressures, fears, threats and hurtful memories. You don't feel free because you are controlled by these forces. Transformation, on the other hand, is a change that begins from the inside and brings freedom and growth into Christlikeness. You feel fulfilled because what you inwardly desire to be is coming to outward expression. You are changing for the better.

What is it that determines whether you will be conformed or transformed? We read in the verse above that you are transformed *"by the renewing of your mind."* Only a renewed mind allows transformation to take place. If you want to experience the life that God desires for you, one that's *"good and acceptable and perfect,"* you will need a renewed mind.

What is a renewed mind? It is a spiritual mind that is influenced and directed by God's Spirit and truth. It is receptive to God's leading and sees life through God's perspective. The unrenewed or natural mind is limited to human reasoning and is crippled by past experiences, disappointments and fear.

Romans 8:7 teaches us that the natural or unrenewed mind *"is hostile to God"* and is *"not even able"* to understand or trust God's ways. It is filled with doubts and fears that keep you from fully obeying God, and therefore it keeps you from the blessings of full obedience. It doesn't accept God's truth and so has a warped view of reality. Its ways end in futility and failure. The natural mind and the renewed mind are in opposition to each other and each strives for control.

Many people find that real change eludes them. The truth is that we will keep doing same things over and over as long as we keep following the ways of our unrenewed mind. Our behavior will only change when our thinking changes. If you can't change your behavior, then you must question your thinking.

A renewed mind brings a total paradigm shift. It operates on a higher level and is able to accept God's ways and thoughts. Isaiah 55:8-9 tells us that God's ways and God's thoughts are not like ours. *"For as the heavens are higher than the earth, so are My ways higher than your ways, and My thoughts than your thoughts"* (Is. 55:9).

An un-renewed mind can't accept God's ways. It will draw back from full obedience. It thinks God's ways are foolish. But what seems foolish to the natural mind is wisdom on a higher level. Only a renewed mind can accept Jesus' life-changing truths like: We find our life by losing it (Matt. 16:25), we become great by becoming a servant (Matt. 20:25-26), we receive by giving (Luke 6:38), and we are elevated as we humble ourselves (Matt. 23:12).

Only a renewed mind allows you to live in God's higher level of understanding. The natural mind sees only the physical world with its limitations and lack, which leads to fear and failure. But the renewed mind sees the invisible reality behind the visible. It sees the hand of God at work and believes and receives from that invisible source.

So how do we gain a renewed mind? First, learn, memorize and meditate on God's Word until it becomes a part of you. Only by seeing life through the perspective of God's Word can we live according to a renewed mind.

Second, yield your mind to Christ. Make a decision to surrender your thoughts before His thoughts. I Corinthians 2:16 says, "We have the mind of Christ." Ask God to inspire your mind as you lay down your own independent thinking.

Finally, yield your will to God's will. There is a close connection between our mind and our will. Our will tends to direct our thinking. Our natural tendency is to rationalize what our will desires.

Until we surrender our will to God, we will struggle to receive God's thoughts. In fact, we will resist them. Every time you face a decision and follow Christ's way, you strengthen your renewed mind. Every decision we make strengthens one mind or the other. The secret to an overcoming life is to live out of a renewed mind.

Prayer – I choose to surrender my natural mind to a renewed mind, one that has been made new by Your Word and Spirit. I want to be receptive to Your leading and see life through Your perspective so that I might receive all the blessings that come from full obedience.

The Joy of the Lord

"Rejoice in the Lord always; again, I will say, rejoice."
Philippians 4:4

Did you know that joy is the primary emotion of the Kingdom of God? The Bible tells us that there is a time for weeping with those who weep & grieving the loss of loved ones, etc. But the underlying emotion is joy. Joy is a sign that the Kingdom of God is being lived out in your life. If you are consistently following God's ways your primary emotion should be joy.

Some people say, "Well, I am not a joyful person by nature, I have a stoic personality type." Well, this joy doesn't have to do with your personality type. In fact, it doesn't even have to do with your circumstances. This is not a joy that only comes when everything turns out just as you hoped.

It is a supernatural joy that comes from God. Romans 14:17 tells us that the Kingdom of God does not consist in religious rules but rather it is a dynamic inward change in the human heart. It says that *"the Kingdom of God is... righteousness, peace and joy **in** the Holy Spirit"* (Rom. 14:17). It is a joy that is "in the Holy Spirit." In other words, it is God's joy that is placed in our heart by the Holy Spirit. This joy is part of the inheritance of every child of God who has been filled with the Holy Spirit. In fact, it is an evidence or fruit of having the Holy Spirit. *"Now the fruit of the Spirit is love, **joy,*** peace, patience, kindness, goodness, faithfulness… " (Gal. 5:22). If I have little joy, I must ask myself if I am neglecting the influence of the Holy Spirit and am instead merely living out of my own wisdom and strength.

Paul's epistle to the Philippians quoted above is known as "the epistle of joy." The word joy in its various forms appears 16 times in its 4 chapters. Paul is so filled with joy that it overflows, "I rejoice and share my joy with you all" (Phil. 2:17). The remarkable thing about this epistle is where it was written. It was written while Paul was in prison and is known as one of the "Prison Epistles." Roman prisons were terrible places but Paul's joy was not based on circumstances. It was "joy in the Holy Spirit." It was a fruit of the Spirit. Fruit is something that comes naturally from a tree that receives water, nutrients and sunlight. Joy is a fruit that comes naturally in us when we live a full Christian life.

Joy lifts us above our troubles. Joy gives us strength to persevere & overcome. Joy is the antidote to sorrow. "Do not be grieved, for the joy of the Lord is your strength" (Nehemiah 8:10). Like rising powerful thermal drafts that allow eagles to "mount up with wings" and soar for great periods above the earth, so joy lifts us up & holds us up.

Getting saved brings great joy! Do you remember the great joy you experienced when you first received Christ? I love to see the joy of new believers. But we can let that joy slip away in our lives. The great Psalmist King David lost his joy due to falling in to sin. He became involved in an adulterous affair. Psalm 51 is his great psalm of repentance. In it, he cries out to God "Restore to me the joy of your salvation" (Ps. 51:12). Many Christians need to pray

David's prayer. Many things can trample out our joy: unconfessed sin, disappointments, doubts and ingratitude. Do you need that prayer? Say it to God "*Restore to me the joy of your salvation.*" Confess and renounce any sin in your life. Thank God for at least 10 blessing you are grateful for   and then worship Him and you will experience His joy.   His joy can be an unceasing fountain bubbling up in your heart. Live today in the strength that His joy gives you.

Prayer - I want Your joy in all circumstances. I want to be strong in the joy of the Lord. Help my attitude to reflect the fruit of the Spirit and the promises of God rather than my circumstances. Restore to me the joy of my salvation.

God's Supply Line

*"Every person is to in subjection to the governing authorities.
For there is no authority except from God….for it is a minister of
God to you for good." Romans 13:1,4*

If one thing marks us as modern Americans, it's a distrust for, and even resentment of, authority. Our culture's negative view of authority has even begun to seep into the church. However, as Christians we understand that God uses authorities as ministers for our good. The words translated "minister" in the verse above is the Greek word *diakinos*, which means servant. It is the same word used for the office of a deacon in the church. All authorities are meant to function as God's representatives through which He brings guidance, protection, wisdom and daily bread into our life. They are God's supply chain. When we respect the authorities God has put in our life, we open up the supply lines from Heaven. But we hinder that supply by resisting or rejecting those authorities.

Beginning at birth, God feeds, clothes, protects and instructs us through our parents. Then He uses teachers to teach us, employers who supply us with money, police who protect us, and church leaders who teach us God's ways and build up His church (this list is not exhaustive). We do not expect money to fall directly from Heaven, lightning bolts to strike those who would harm us or to be "raptured" out of a burning building. We recognize that God uses delegated authorities to do those things. This means that if we refuse to accept the authorities God places over us, we cut off God's supply and protection. The teen who rebels against her parents forfeits the wisdom, love and protection God would bring through them. The employee who disrespects and poorly serves his employer will soon find he has cut off God's source of supply and will suffer lack.

This remains true even if the authority is very imperfect. We must be able to look beyond the flawed authority figure and see God as our Source standing behind them. Because of free will, authorities may become corrupted and self-serving. However, if our attitude to authority remains right, God will be faithful to bring us what we need, often using the self-serving authority despite himself (Prov. 21:1). In fact, flawed authorities can serve as tests to reveal whether there is pride or rebellion in our heart, *"Servants be submissive to your masters with all respect, not only to those who good and gentle, but also to those who are unreasonable. For this finds favor, if for the sake of conscience toward God a person bears up under sorrows when suffering unjustly"* (I Peter 12:18-19). We respect and obey a delegated authority because they carry God's authority, not because they have earned our respect (and when we do so, it brings God's favor upon us). But while showing them respect, we do not follow them in doing evil because we have a higher authority we must obey. Authorities receive their authority from God, so when they are in rebellion to God, they lose their authority in the area of their rebellion and need not be obeyed. But remember, even ungodly and wicked governors and mayors still serve God by providing us with order and protection against criminals. Therefore, we must show them honor and obey them to the extent possible, for God's sake.

Just as there is authority in the family, society and the workplace so God has established authority in the church for the benefit of the saints (Eph. 4:8,11-2). When we respect the office and anointing God has put on His leaders, we are protected and blessed. The Bible addresses those in the Church, *"Obey your leaders and submit to* them, for they keep watch over your souls as those who will give an account. Let them do this with joy and not with grief, for this would be unprofitable for you" (Heb. 13:17). We submit to church leaders for our own profit. When we refuse to do so, we lose the profit God wants to give us. The reason that church leaders are accountable to God for giving oversight and keeping watch over the souls of others, is because they have received authority, gifting and anointing from God to do so. When we recognize and accept this, it opens doors of blessing and supply to us. I have noticed that when someone comes to me, respecting the office of a pastor and expecting God to bring His supply through me, that God honors their faith. I can literally "feel" God's wisdom, counsel and power flow through me to them. However, if they do not have respect for the office and anointing of a pastor, I sit there empty, with little to say and nothing profitable to give them. Submitting to authority is more than just avoiding direct rebellion. It is an attitude that seeks out the advice and blessing of the authority, because you recognize that God will bring you His wisdom and supply through them.

Remember, God has placed authority in the family, society and church to protect us and bring us His supply. Being under authority is a blessing and not a curse. They are God's servants to bring His riches into our life. How is your relationship to authorities in your life? Do you see them as a blessing? Do you consult with them or do you avoid them? Do you need to ask God to help you change any attitudes?

Prayer - Thank You for bringing authorities into my life to be Your channels of blessing and protection. Help me to honor them for Your sake, so that I may receive the fullness of Your wisdom, guidance and supply offered to me through them.

Growing in God's Favor

*"And Jesus kept increasing in wisdom and stature
and in favor with God and men." Luke 2:52*

Following the story of Jesus in the Temple at age 12, we read that He returned to Nazareth. And as our text tell us, "*He kept increasing in…. favor with God and men.*" To have favor means you are held in favorable regard. You hold a privileged position and you receive preferred treatment. It is great to have favor with men, but it's far greater to have favor with God. It's true that Jesus was born with God's favor. But it is also true that He increased in favor with God. Likewise, when we are born again, we have God's favor. But it is also true that we can grow in His favor. It's wonderful to realize that we can grow in favor with God. The prophet Samuel learned this as a young boy. I Samuel 2:26 reads, "*Now the boy Samuel was growing in stature and in favor both with the Lord and with men.*"

The 12 disciples observed that God's favor was poured out on Jesus. They wondered how they could have God's favor on them. So they observed Him closely for three years. If you study the gospels, you will find that the disciples made two important requests of Jesus. In Luke 11:1 they said, "*Lord, teach us to pray.*" And on the last night in the upper room after Jesus told them He would no longer be with them; they made the second request. Philip, as spokesman for the group, said, "*Lord, show us the Father, and it is enough for us*" (John 14:8). After closely studying

Jesus, they had made a discovery. Jesus' life of favor flowed out from His experience of God as His Father, which He enjoyed in His private life of prayer and devotion.

They had observed the priority Jesus placed on this time with His Father. No matter how many or how pressing the demands, Jesus would sneak away to be with His Father (Luke 5:15-16). Often He would spend whole nights in prayer. Once when Jesus saw the Pharisees making a great show of their prayers Jesus had told them, *"But when you pray, go into your room and shut the door and pray to your Father who is in secret. And your Father who sees in secret will reward you"* (Matt. 6:6 ESV). Jesus said that God has a reward waiting for you in the secret place with Him. Do you want to experience God as your Father like Jesus did? Jesus said your Father is waiting for you in the secret place. Where is that secret place? It is a place you build through personal prayer and Bible study and mediation. It's a place where you grow in unshakeable confidence in God and love for Him.

There are three people waiting for you in the secret place. The first is your Heavenly Father. Jesus said He is waiting for you there to reward you. The next is the person you are now. Standing alone before your Father and in the Light of His Word you will see yourself as God sees you. The third is the person you can become-that's the person that only God can make you.

You honor someone when you give them your full and undivided attention. When we honor God in this way, we grow in His favor. People say they are just too busy to have a devotional life with God. What they are saying is they are too busy to grow in God's favor and blessing. Everyone always has time for what they consider most important. For some, prayer is just going down a list of requests, for others it is a time of enjoying their Heavenly Father and drawing life and strength from Him just like Jesus did. If you do likewise, that time will become the foundation for your life. And you will be transformed. God is waiting for you in the secret place.

Prayer - I want to honor You and grow in Your favor. Help me to truly value and prioritize my time alone with You. Help me to find the time and place where I can meet with You every day in Bible reading, meditation and prayer.

Day 16

Overcoming Discouragement

"But David strengthened Himself in the Lord." I Samuel 30:6

You may have heard that Thomas Edison's first 2000 attempts at creating the light bulb failed before he achieved success. Abraham Lincoln suffered a number of business and political defeats in his early life. Dr. Seuss' first book for children was turned down by 27 publishers. Much of what we enjoy today wouldn't exist if people were not able to overcome failures, setbacks and discouragement. All of us get discouraged and knocked down by life, but all of us can recover, make a comeback and finish strong.

David was anointed by Samuel to be King, defeated Goliath and was a great warrior. But then came a number of betrayals and false accusations and as a result he spent years as a fugitive running from King Saul. Finally, while living at Ziklag, the Amalakites carried off his and his men's wives and children while they were away. His men spoke of stoning him. It was the lowest point of His life. David had come to the end of his strength. But then he *"strengthened himself in the Lord."* He trusted in a strength greater than His own. David recovered all those who had been carried off with the Lord's help. Soon after, King Saul died and David became King and built a great Kingdom.

All of us deal with discouragement at times. Sometimes it's because we have unrealistic ideas about how things are and therefore, we have illusions about how easy things will be. These lead to unrealistic expectations of how things will turn out and when they don't turn out as we hoped we become discouraged and disillusioned. Everyone starts out with illusions and unrealistic expectations. Don't become discouraged and give up when they fail to happen. God can use that experience in our life. He wants to take us on a journey from illusions and unrealistic expectations to greater maturity and achievement. Sometimes we get discouraged because of delays and setbacks. Prov. 13:12 says, *"Hope deferred makes the heart sick, but desire fulfilled is a tree of life."* We all know the joy and energy we get from reaching a goal. Delays and setbacks do the opposite. They drain our enthusiasm and tempt us to think that our goal is not obtainable. But delays don't necessarily mean God isn't for our goal. God often uses delays and setbacks to prepare us. I almost quit the ministry after a great disappointment thinking God hadn't called me. But actually, it was one of my most important times of preparation.

Sometimes I think that the Devil's main job is not so much to tempt us to do wrong, as it is to discourage us from doing right. If he can discourage you by exaggerating the size of the obstacles and make you doubt God's promises, he can defeat you and cause you walk away from your God given goals. He whispers in our ear, *"It's hopeless, God didn't call you to this."* But God can give you a second wind and you can finish strong and triumphant.

Every set back and failure is an opportunity for us to reexamine our goal. This is important because God won't help us reach wrong goals. So, the first thing we should do is go to God in prayer and talk to mature spiritual people for counsel. If, after doing so, you are convinced God wants you to move forward you can rise up strengthened with fresh conviction. Someone said once that failure is just an opportunity to begin again with greater understanding and insight. Next, ask, "Am I truly building with God as my foundation? Where am I drawing my strength and direction from? Am I putting my confidence in my own wisdom or am I drawing it from God?" In order to succeed you need a Source greater than yourself. If necessary, deal with wrong motives, wrong attitudes and sin because these will hinder God's working through us. Make sure you are doing the things that build you up spiritually. Finally, having done all of the above, practice diligence. Hebrews 10:36 says, "*For you have need of endurance* (diligent perseverance) *so that when you have done the will of God, you may receive what was promised.*" Diligence is a requirement for success. My brother David and I searched for 3 ½ years and looked at many dozens of buildings before we found one, we could rent for our church to meet in. Believe me, we grew discouraged. But at the end we found a building in the area that God wanted us to be in (not our first choice) with the right landlord, and that single building eventually grew into an entire campus. Diligence ensures that you will not quit before you have learned the lessons God wants to teach you and have been fully prepared for God's provision.

Like King David, all of us battle discouragement at times. One moment all seemed lost. But soon everything began to change and David built a great kingdom. The circumstances didn't change, God didn't change, but David changed. He "*strengthened himself in the Lord.*" We get discouraged by looking at circumstances and listening to bad reports but we gain strength by looking to God and remembering His promises.

Prayer - Help me to always look to You as my Source. Help me to put away foolish self-confidence and unrealistic expectations and to have godly goals and right motives. Teach me to look to You rather then be intimidated by circumstances so that I might be strong in the Lord.

Day 17

Strong in the Lord Part 1

*"Finally, be strong in the Lord and in the strength of His might.
Put on the full armor of God, so that you will be able to stand
firm against the schemes of the devil. For our struggle is not
against flesh and blood, but against the rulers, against the
powers, against the world forces of this darkness, against the
spiritual forces of wickedness in the heavenly places."*
Ephesians 6:10-12

Struggle is a part of life. Everyone feels like they are in a battle sometimes, and all of us feel the need for greater strength. Unfortunately, most of us tend to try to win the battle by our own wits and our own strength. But God doesn't call us to battle in our own strength, but rather in His. He doesn't call us to serve Him in our own strength, but rather in His.

The above passage begins by calling us to be strong, not in our strength but in His. We are to *"be strong in the Lord, and the strength of His might."* God wants us to rise up out of our human weakness and put on His strength. Too many of us experience failure in relationships, in overcoming habitual sins, or in overcoming conflicts. It is usually because we are depending upon our own strength and wisdom. Overcomers have learned to overcome by God's strength. We do not gain the Lord's strength by being passive. We are directed to *"be strong in the Lord's might."* We have a part to play. To be strong in the Lord is a process that we learn; it is a skill that we grow in.

To do this we must recognize the true arena of our conflict. We learn that ultimately *"our struggle is not against flesh and blood"* but against the devil's schemes (and his demons). Our struggle is against the lies, intimidation, and deception of the enemy. These bring about unbelief, doubt, fear and compromise within us. Your problem isn't a lack of finances. Don't you know God has promised to supply your every need? Your problem isn't that the task ahead of you is too great, for the Bible promises us, *"I can do all things through Christ who strengthens me"* (Phil. 4:13 NKJV). Our real problem is that we have been deceived by the devil so that doubt, unbelief and fear cut us off from God's supply. Your real enemy isn't that person who opposes you, but the lies of the world and spiritual influence that hold and direct that individual. These can only be overcome by the Lord's power and weapons.

Until we focus on the right arena, we will not have the Lord's strength to overcome. If we are fussing and fighting with people, then our attention is in the wrong arena. If we get down on ourselves because we feel inadequate, then our attention is in the wrong arena. In every challenge and every conflict, we must ask ourselves, "What is the spiritual issue that is before me?" Do you need to forgive, turn the other cheek and *"bless those who persecute you"* (Rom. 12:14)? Instead of hoarding in fear, do you need to *"give, (so) it will be given to you... a good measure – pressed down, shaken together, and running over"* (Luke 6:38)? In every instance we must reject the devil's lie and follow God's direction, and we will gain the victory.

Next, we must use the Lord's armor and weapons. In the next verse following our passage above, we are told to *"take up the full armor of God"* (Eph. 6:13). God has given us armor and weapons so that by them we can resist the devil, stand firm and overcome him. This armor is listed in Ephesians 6:14-18. We will look at these weapons in the next two meditations. In studying them, we will learn more about the provision God has given us to overcome.

All of us face difficulties and mistreatment. We are not to react to them in the flesh. Our assignment is to focus on the true arena of our conflict, prayerfully determine the spiritual issue that is facing us, and then put on the Lord's strength by following His Word and putting on His armor. Remember, it is our heritage as children of God to overcome all the devil's schemes. His weapons will not be effective against us (Is. 54:17). As born-again believers, we will overcome him because *"greater is He who is in you than he who is in the world"* (I John 4:4). Whatever lies ahead of you this day you can face in confidence, if only you will be strong in the Lord and the strength of His might.

Prayer – I want to overcome in Your strength rather than struggle in my own. Help me to always recognize the true arenas of my conflict. Help me to use Your weapons and strategy to overcome.

Day 18

Strong in the Lord Part 2

"Therefore take up the whole armor of God that you may be able to withstand in the evil day, and having done all, to stand firm. Stand therefore, having fastened on the belt of truth, and having put on the breastplate of righteousness, and, as shoes for your feet, having put on the readiness given by the gospel of peace." Ephesians 6:13-15 (ESV)

We learned in the previous meditation that God has given us armor and weapons to defeat the devil and overcome his schemes. In today's passage, we come to the first three of our weapons. But, first, we must note that Satan also has armor. In Luke 11:20-22 Jesus teaches us that Satan relies on his armor to protect his possessions. But Jesus is stronger and removes Satan's armor and sets the captives free. What is Satan's armor that keeps people bound? It is the exact opposite of God's armor that protects us. We will see this as we go through the list of God's armor.

BELT OF TRUTH
The first item in our armor is *"the belt of truth."* This refers to ancient warriors tying up their loose flowing garments into their wide belt so they wouldn't be restricted by them or trip over them while fighting. The most important thing for any fighter is to have sure footing in order to keep their balance. If we are to stand firm, we must have God's true (biblical) views in every area of life. Satan's armor, therefore, is to fill us with wrong beliefs and

worldly lies by which he can trip us up and bind us. Our first protection, then, is that we must commit ourselves to God's truth in every area of life. We must become committed students of His Word. We must be accountable to others who will speak God's truth to us in love when we begin to stray.

BREASTPLATE OF RIGHTEOUSNESS

Our next protection is *"the breastplate of righteousness."* The breastplate is the armor that protects your chest and heart. Putting on the breastplate means we commit ourselves to righteousness or right living before the Lord. If we live lives of unrighteousness, compromise and sin, we expose our heart to the arrows of condemnation, guilt and doubt from Satan. We will not have confidence before God, but will draw back from Him in shame. If we try to live rightly, then we will rest confidently in Christ's righteousness which covers us and by which we overcome our enemy. I John 3:21 says, *"If our heart does not condemn us, we have confidence before God."* Satan holds us by getting us to live unrighteously, and then binding us in shame and guilt. That is why it is so critical for us to confess our sins to God, receive forgiveness and then put on the breastplate of righteousness.

SHOES

The next part of our spiritual gear is our shoes. We read that our readiness to share the gospel should be *"as shoes for your feet."* The CEV translations reads, *"Your desire to tell the good news about peace should be like shoes on your feet."* I call these our "gospel shoes." Now what does this mean? In the Bible, shoes often refer to our lifestyle or purpose. Our feet direct our path. They direct us to certain places and away from others. They direct our journey. In the same way, our purpose determines the choices we make and the paths we select. If our purpose is to make Jesus' good news known and to extend His Kingdom, we will not wander from God's path. Rather than wandering into Satan's traps, we will keep to the path that brings us into God's blessings. If Satan can get us to choose some other purpose, such as pursuing wealth, worldly pursuits, or pleasure, then we will wander from God's path. What is your overarching purpose in life? Is it to spread Jesus' gospel and Kingdom? Let your "gospel shoes" direct your path.

So many Christians think of themselves as consumers who window shop through life and sample things, and then choose the things that they think will make them happy. But God did not call us to be consumers, but rather warriors, who join Jesus in the battle, share in His victories and enjoy the blessings. To enable us to know victory, He has given us His armor, and He calls us to *"be strong in the Lord and in the strength of His might."* (Eph. 6:10).

Prayer – I want to overcome Satan and walk in the pathways of Your blessings. With Your help, I commit myself wholeheartedly to Your truth, to living by Your standards of righteousness, and to be consistently focused on my purpose as a disciple of Jesus Christ.

Day 19

Strong in the Lord Part 3

"In addition to all, taking up the shield of faith with which you will be able to extinguish all the flaming arrows of the evil one. And take THE HELMET OF SALVATION, and the sword of the Spirit, which is the word of God. With all prayer and petition pray at all times in the Spirit, and with this in view, be on the alert with all perseverance and petition for all the saints." Ephesians 6:16-18

We have been studying the armor of God. This armor is our spiritual defense against attacks by Satan. This armor corresponds to the typical armor of the Roman soldier. It allows us to stand firm and overcome our adversary. Having looked at the first four pieces in the previous lesson, we will now address the remaining three.

SHIELD OF FAITH
Our fourth piece of armor is *"the shield of faith."* A Roman soldier would hold up his shield to protect himself from arrows. When Satan attacks us, our faith in Christ protects us. If your trust is fully in God, you will not be panicked or set aflame by the devil's schemes or threats. II Corinthians 5:7 reminds us that, *"we walk by faith, not by sight."* When we live in reaction to circumstances and threats, we are vulnerable to the devil's schemes. Satan wants to freeze us in doubt and unbelief. But when we live according to our trust and faith in God, then we can ignore the devil's threats because we are steadied by God's promises. When we trust in His promises, they guard us, guide us and protect us from doubt.

HELMET OF SALVATION

The fifth piece of armor we are told to put on is *"the helmet of salvation."* The helmet protects our head – that is our mind, thoughts and imagination. Satan wants to fill our mind and imagination with confusion, doubt, fear and indecision, in order to keep us from God's purposes. But God gives us a helmet of salvation or a "renewed mind" – one that is made new by the Holy Spirit (Rom. 12:2). A renewed mind is a spiritual mind that is at peace and in tune with God. It is a mind that is responsive to the Holy Spirit. It allows you to live above the uncertainties, pressures and threats of this world because it is settled on God's Word.

Satan's armor works to keep us in our natural or fleshly mind, which doubts and resists God's ways. Romans 8:7 (NIV) tells us *"The mind governed by the flesh is hostile to God; it does not submit to God's law, nor can it do so."* Our natural or carnal mind would rather justify ourselves than repent. It prefers living by our own wits rather than looking to God in trust. We put on the renewed mind as we think and meditate on God's Word, pray as we go through the day, and regularly reflect on the Lord's love and faithfulness. In this way we are protected from Satan's deception.

SWORD OF THE SPIRIT

As is often pointed out, the sixth item, *"the sword of the Spirit"* is an offensive weapon as well as defensive. It can not only deflect a blow, but it can also inflict one. We are told that this sword is the Word of God. We use it defensively to assure our hearts when we are under attack, and also offensively, to attack Satan's kingdom by setting captives free through preaching, teaching and deliverance. The word translated as "word" here is *rhema*, which includes both words of scripture and also words of knowledge and revelation by the Holy Spirit. Jesus quoted scripture when tempted by the devil, and also to defend Himself against charges by the Pharisees. He used words of knowledge often in His ministry to save and deliver people, such as with the Samaritan woman at the well (John 4:16-19). We become powerful as we know and use God's Word.

PRAYER
Our final piece of armor is prayer. We are told to *"pray at all times in the Spirit."* Prayer is essential to spiritual warfare. II Corinthians 10:4 states that our weapons are *"mighty through God"* (KJV) or *"divinely powerful"* (NASB). Our armor and weapons are enhanced as we ask God to empower them. We pray not just for ourselves, but we also pray for others, to reject Satan's armor and put on the full armor of God.

God has given us wonderful armor and weapons so that we can *"be strong in the Lord and in the strength of His might"* (Eph. 6:10). God does not call us to be strong in ourselves, but to learn to put on His strength. It is your inheritance to overcome the enemy, and God has given you armor and weapons to do so. So put on your heavenly armor every day.

Prayer – Help me to put on and trust in Your spiritual armor every day. Teach me to be quick to recognize when Satan is trying to put his armor on me so I can resist him and keep it off. Help me to meditate upon Your truth and be sensitive to Your Spirit, and teach me to pray in the Spirit for myself and others, so I can be strong in the Lord.

It's Better to Be Blessed

"...for you were called for this very purpose that you might inherit a blessing." I Peter 3:9

On Jan 28, 1986, at 11:38 am, the Space Shuttle Challenger lifted off from Cape Kennedy in Florida. Seventy-three seconds later it blew up while millions of Americans watched on television. All seven astronauts were killed. After recovering the wreckage, scientists determined that the explosion happened because a small rubber sealing ring, only ¼ inch in diameter, had failed and leaked rocket fuel which caused the explosion. Sometimes small things really matter.

Sometimes making a small adjustment in our lives can make a profound change. I want you to consider one simple four-word sentence that can totally change your life. *"Pursue blessedness over happiness."* It is better to be blessed than to be happy. Most people are preoccupied with trying to be happy. It is their greatest motivation in life. For many, everything boils down to one question, *"What do I think will make me happy?"* But happiness is a transitory feeling that can slip through your fingers. It depends upon changing circumstances. It is fragile. One accident, one phone call, one report from a doctor can shatter it. But God's blessing endures. God's blessing is a favored status. It means that God's favor rests on you and God's Face is turned toward you. It means that God will strengthen you in every battle and comfort you in every sorrow. It means that His wisdom and power will guide you, uphold you and advance your best interests.

Being blessed is not out of reach. In fact, our opening verse states that we were called for this purpose. God spoke through the prophet Isaiah, *"Therefore the Lord longs to be gracious to you. How blessed are all those who long for Him"* (Is. 30:18). What a wonderful truth! When we truly long for the Lord, then He will do what He longs to do - which is to bless us. Our culture teaches us to be obsessed with happiness but blessedness is far more important and far better. The Bible speaks about blessedness over 400 times but only mentions happiness 21 times.

It's true that a blessed person will generally be happy but they are not the same thing. For instance, you can be happy (at least temporarily) without being blessed. You can be having fun and yet be deceived about how things will turn out. Sin can bring temporary happiness but always ends in sorrow. You can also be blessed and yet temporarily unhappy. I have a friend, who some years ago, had their young son killed by a reckless drunk driver in front of their house. Although they were in great sorrow, he said to me, "The comfort and peace of God is more than you can imagine. I am surrounded by Christian friends and God is meeting every need." When you can experience the worst that life can hand you and still have comfort, peace and even joy you are blessed. *Happiness is a feeling that can be easily lost, but blessedness is a condition or state that God places us in that no event or person can take from us.*

For many people, happiness involves the *pursuit of things* and the using of people and events to serve our agenda. And since we often can't control people or events it often leads to disappointments, conflicts, and even broken relationships. But blessedness is different. Blessedness involves the *pursuit of God* which includes serving others. These build love and harmony.

God can do for us far beyond what we could ever do for ourselves if only we would seek Him. In Deuteronomy 28 God lists great blessings He wanted to give Israel. It includes this wonderful promise/principal, *"All these blessings shall come upon you and overtake you if you obey the Lord your God"* (Deut. 28:2). As you pursue God, the blessings of God pursue and overtake you. I have pursued both happiness and blessedness in my life. I learned that in pursuing blessedness, I received both blessedness and happiness. Pursuing happiness however brought me neither. Many people, in pursuing their happiness, disqualify themselves from blessedness because in so doing they make choices that dishonor God and go against His Word. I can't control my happiness because I can't control my circumstances or how others treat me. But I can control whether I will be blessed because I can control my actions.

The Bible is full of pathways to blessedness. For instance, Proverb 28:20 says, *"A faithful man will abound with blessings."* I can't control my circumstances but I can endeavor to be faithful to my family, my church, my responsibilities and my God. If I do so, I will be blessed. Psalm 41:1 says, *"How blessed is he who considers the helpless."* I can't control my happiness but I can be compassionate to those in need and if I do so, I will be blessed. Malachi 3:10 says *"Bring the whole tithe... and test me now in this"* says the Lord of hosts, *"if I will not open for you the windows of heaven and pour out for you a blessing until it overflows."* I want the blessed life, so I will tithe. I can't control my happiness but I can tithe. Those who say they can't afford to tithe are really saying that they can't afford to be blessed. Anyone can tithe because 90% with the Lord's blessing is more than 100% without it. Happiness is fleeting, but blessedness endures. Blessings multiply and increase on top of each other.

Prayer - Help me to pursue blessedness instead of happiness. I want to pursue You so You will pursue me with Your blessings. Help me to walk in the pathways of blessedness rather than in the ways of this world.

Day 21

Seeing and Entering

"The time is fulfilled and the Kingdom of God is at hand; repent and believe in the gospel." Mark 1:15

While some people think that the Kingdom of God is entirely in the future, Jesus taught in the verse above that, because of His coming to earth, it is available today. In other words, Jesus said, that the time has come, the Kingdom is at hand (within your reach) so change your thinking and way of living. For many believers, the Kingdom of God is largely a mystery. If you ask them to define it, they could not. It's like a closed book they may have paged through but never read. The Pharisee, Nicodemus, was familiar with religion but not with the Kingdom or its power. When he witnessed Jesus' ministry, he was astonished. He came to Jesus by night to enquire of Jesus' secret. Jesus said to him, *"Truly, truly I say to you, unless one is born again, he cannot see the Kingdom of God"* (John 3:3). Before Nicodemus could see the Kingdom, He would have to be born again.

Most of us have heard many sermons on this verse and generally they are about the need to be born again. But this verse is really about *seeing the Kingdom*. Being born again is the means to that end. People who haven't been born again can't perceive the Kingdom. That's why they don't understand how you, a Christian, think or what you do. They say, "Why do you give so much money to church? Why do you take all this religious stuff so seriously?" They don't understand you because they can't see what you see. It's like being awake in a room full of sleeping people. They are not conscious of the fact that they are asleep, nor that you are awake, but you are aware of both.

63

But Jesus went on to say much more just two verses later, *"Truly, truly I say to you, unless one is born of water and the Spirit he cannot enter the Kingdom of God"* (John 3:5). Note what Jesus revealed to Nicodemus. Beyond just SEEING the Kingdom, you can ENTER it. Being born again merely enables you to see the Kingdom; it doesn't mean that you will fully enter it. To be able to see the Kingdom is one thing but to enter it is another. It is one thing to believe that God can do a miracle but it's another thing to experience one. It's one thing to believe that God can heal, deliver and save others but it's another to be an instrument that He uses to do so. Many people have felt the Presence and conviction of God when they visited a church, but they went no further. They didn't repent and take their first steps into the Kingdom. Many people accept Christ and receive forgiveness but, through a lack of faith or desire, do not proceed any farther. It is what separates overcoming Christians from nominal and defeated Christians.

Jesus said that if we would seek first the Kingdom and its righteousness (its reign and rule), that all good and needed things would be given us (Matt. 6:33). So how do we enter the Kingdom more fully? Jesus told His disciples, *"To you it has been granted to know the mysteries of the Kingdom of Heaven"* (Matt. 13:11). We cannot enter the Kingdom unless we know its mysteries. These mysteries or secrets are revealed in the Bible and especially in the teaching of Jesus. Jesus told Peter, *"I will give you the keys to the Kingdom of Heaven; and whatever you bind on earth shall have been bound in Heaven, and whatever you loose on earth will have been loosed in Heaven"* (Matt. 16:19). When Jesus promised Peter the keys, He was promising him more than just authority; He was promising him teaching that would allow him to release the power and riches of this Kingdom (the only other time Jesus used the word "key" in the NT, He was clearly speaking of teaching and knowledge (Luke 11:52).

By following these teachings Peter (and others) would be able to link heavens power and supply to earthly situations. These mysteries or keys go against human thinking and must be entered into by faith. For instance, Jesus taught that we become great by humbling ourselves and being a servant, and that we receive blessings by first giving to others. We examine many of these mysteries or keys throughout this devotional book. In addition, in my book "Unlocking the Kingdom" (available on Amazon, Kindle and Audible), we examine 13 of these most powerful mysteries in depth.

These principles are sometimes call "spiritual laws." The same Creator who operates the physical world through great natural laws also does the same in the spiritual realm. God is consistent. He is a God of order and laws. When we learn to abide by these laws in both the physical and spiritual realms, we prosper. This means that the abundance and possibilities of the Kingdom become available to those who follow God's spiritual laws, in the same way that the natural world has yielded its riches as we have learned and followed the great laws of nature. We greatly impoverish ourselves when we do not carefully study God's Word but greatly empower and enrich ourselves when we know and follow His Word.

It is the right of every born-again Christian not only to see the Kingdom but to enter it. God wants you to live in the power and supply of His invisible Kingdom. God wants us to move forward confidently in His Kingdom, *"Do not be afraid, little flock, for your Father has chosen gladly to give you the Kingdom"* (Luke 12:32).

Prayer - Thank You for gladly giving me the Kingdom. I want to fully enter and live in it in every situation. Help me to study Your Word diligently and obey it, so that I might be an instrument of Your Kingdom.

The Power of a Promise

"O Lord, who may abide in Your tent? Who may dwell on Your holy hill? He who walks with integrity, and works righteousness, and speaks truth in his heart...He swears to his own hurt and does not change." Psalm 1-2, 4

A movie starring Nicholas Cage entitled "It Could Happen to You" tells the true story of NYPD policeman Robert Cunningham. He was finishing a meal at his favorite restaurant and jokingly asked Phyllis Penza, who had waited on him for 7 years, if she would rather receive a tip from him or get half of his winnings should his ticket win in the New York lotto. She smiled and said she would take the winnings. His ticket won 6 million dollars the next day and he kept his promise. It cost him 3 million dollars to honor his word.

Our passage asks who may fellowship with God? To whom will God reveal Himself? All of God's friends are promise keepers. They keep their word even when it's not to their advantage. If you want to walk with God, you must be a person of your word.

As a person you will be defined by the promises you make and keep. If you were to ask me who I am, I would answer that I am a follower of Christ, a husband, a father and a pastor. I am those things because of promises I made and kept. Likewise, your life will be defined by the promises you make and keep or don't keep. Making and keeping promises brings order, security, hope and blessing to others. Breaking promises does the opposite. Breaking a marriage vow brings pain, distress and uncertainty to a spouse and children. Broken promises can bring devastation. Since everything in life depends upon promises being kept, God holds us accountable for our promises (Prov. 19:9; Malachi 2:12-13). Therefore, we should not make promises lightly, and only when we fully intend to keep them.

The first place we need to keep and honor our word is to God. God considers our promises made to Him as sacred and binding (Num. 30:12). Sometimes people pray to God in difficult times and make vows and promises to God if He will help them. Then, when God answers their prayer and things work out or ease up, they neglect their promise to God. This is foolish and is tempting God. Rather we should say with the Psalmist, King David, *"I shall pay you my vows, which my lips uttered and my mouth spoke when I was in distress"* (Ps. 66: 13b-14).

One way in which God differs from us is that He always keeps His word. Israel's existence depended on it, *"I, the Lord do not change. So you, descendants of Jacob, are not destroyed"* (Malachi 3:6). The reason Israel did not pass away like other nations wasn't because Israel was better than other nations. It was because God had made a promise to Jacob's grandfather, Abraham, and God doesn't change. In the same way, God promised King David that his descendants would always sit on the Throne of Israel. He guaranteed this promise by stating a truth about Himself, *"My covenant I will not violate, nor will I alter the utterance of My lips"* (Ps.89:34). David's descendants sat on the throne for 22 generations. Despite the wickedness and failure of many of Judah's kings, the throne remained in David's family until Jesus,

David's descendent, assumed the throne for all time. All because God had given David His word. God's faithfulness to His word is why we can base our salvation on His promise (John 3:16, etc.). In fact, almost everything we do as Christians we do because of some promise God has made to us in the Bible. As His children, God wants us to honor our word just as He does.

God equates His word with His name, *"For You have magnified Your word according to all Your name"* (Ps. 138:2). God says that His name is only as good as His word. God's reputation is built on keeping His word. It is the same with us. If your word is no good, than neither is your name. Many people today are in the habit of not honoring their word or following through on what they say. Do people consider you a person who keeps your word? The greatest poverty is when a person's word and name have no worth. Proverbs 22:1 says, *"A good name is to be more desired than great riches."* You can always make more money but what do you do when people stop trusting you or believing your words? You are never too young to begin building a good name, and you are never too old to change your reputation by keeping your word and doing what you say.

The world is built and held together by people who make promises and keep them. Every good thing you have is because somebody somewhere made a promise and kept it. If you are a person of your word, then you have great power. In 1942, General MacArthur and the US forces had to withdraw from the Philippines before the advancing Japanese. For 2 years the Filipinos endured Japanese occupation strengthened by MacArthur's promise, "I shall return."

Today many people run from making promises. By doing so they impoverish themselves. You are enlarged by making commitments and keeping them. You are diminished by avoiding commitments or breaking them. You can only have a life of fulfilment and joy by making and keeping promises. Even if you didn't have anything else in the world, you would still have your word. And when you keep it, you enrich the world and you can be a friend of God.

Prayer - I thank You that You always keep Your word. Your faithfulness is my salvation and security. Help me to keep my word to You and others, so that I might enrich the world and truly be Your friend.

Beware of Leaven

"Under these circumstances, after so many thousands of people had gathered together that they there stepping on one another, He began saying to His disciples, 'Beware of the leaven of the Pharisees, which is hypocrisy.'" Luke 12:1

Jesus and His disciples were wildly successful and in great demand. Everyone was giving them great accolades and hanging on their every word. They were sought out and given gifts. In this context Jesus gives them a warning, *"Beware of the leaven of the Pharisees which is hypocrisy."* Because acceptance and popularity can fill a need in us and make us feel good, it brings a danger. The danger is that we begin to put on a front and play-act in order to keep being accepted and approved. Appearances become most important: How do I look to others? What do others think of me? What do I have to do to fit in? Hypocrisy is more intent on outward perception rather than inward reality. In the previous chapter, Jesus said to the Pharisees, *"Now you Pharisees clean the outside of the cup and of the platter; but inside of you, you are full of robbery and wickedness"* (Luke 11:39).

Spiritual hypocrisy happens when we care more about what people think about us than how we appear to God. Jesus compares it to leaven (yeast), because, like yeast, hypocrisy grows until it has corrupted everything (Gal. 5:9). If you let a little hypocrisy into your life, it will grow until it has corrupted every part of your life. It can even corrupt a whole church. The root cause of this hypocrisy is when we seek our security and self-worth from people rather than from God. If you seek your acceptance and approval (glory) from people, then you won't seek them wholeheartedly from God, and you will be cut off from growing in faith. Jesus said to the Pharisees, *"How can you believe, when you receive glory from one another and you do not see the glory that is from God?"* (John 5:44)

I've watched this play out for years among many young people who attended our youth groups. From the outside they appeared to be followers of Christ (and no doubt they considered themselves such). But after graduating from high school, they went away to college, joined the military, or just moved away and many dropped out of the Christian life. They had lived for acceptance and approval in the youth group rather than pursued true and lasting transformation in Christ. They were at church, but they were largely seeking after the wrong prize. They sought the prize of human acceptance and approval and never became rooted in God. Then, when they left and became a part of a different group, they conformed to that one. They were like the seed in the parable of the sower that never developed deep roots (Matt. 13:5-6).

There are two types of fellowship available at church. There is the horizontal or social fellowship with people and there is the vertical fellowship with God. The horizontal is good and important, but it can't substitute for the vertical fellowship with God, which must be primary. If you primarily go to church and small group in order to see your friends rather than pursue God, you should change that. Hebrews 11:6 says that God is our rewarder. If we look for our reward anywhere else, it is idolatry and real faith is blocked. At the church where I was saved when I was 23, I was very popular and respected. The students in my youth group greatly admired me, and all the approval became an idol in my heart. God had to take me away to a liberal seminary in the Midwest so I would learn that there is nothing more precious or rewarding than God.

It's foolish to care more about what people see on the outside than what God sees on the inside. Why do we work so hard to hide from people what we are not afraid for God to see? The conformity trap happens when we believe our greatest need is to be accepted by others. There were many Jews in Jesus' day who were only secret followers of Jesus because, *"they loved the approval of men rather than the approval of God"* (John 12:43). Why do we pursue the reward of human acceptance over the rewards that only God can give? His rewards are infinitely greater.

God wants to give us a vibrant inner life in union with the Holy Spirit. When we set aside distractions and idols and pursue God with all our heart, we find His fellowship, joy, freedom and power. Check your priorities and motivations as a Christian. Our Father created us in His own image and likeness so we might relate directly to Him. As we increasingly make God our highest pursuit, we will find that He is our unfailing source of security, identity and happiness. If we will seek God above everything else, He has promised us a reward (Matt. 6:1-4).

Prayer – You are my great rewarder and the prize I seek. I thank You for every blessing You give, including a church family and ministry, but I seek You above them all. You are my unfailing source and in You I trust. May the motivations and intent of my heart be pleasing to You.

Crossing in a Storm

"Immediately He made the disciples get into the boat and go ahead of Him to the other side, while He sent the crowds away."
Matthew 14:22

After feeding the 5000, Jesus told his disciples to get into a boat and go to the other side of the Sea of Galilee, where He would meet them. What He didn't think necessary to tell them was what they would encounter on the way. On the way they would encounter a great storm. In the storm the disciples became afraid they would perish. Jesus came to them, walking on the water, in the midst of the storm. He calmed the storm and said to them, *"You of little faith, why did you doubt?"* (Matt. 14:31). Jesus had told them that He would meet them on the other side. Why were they afraid and upset? Jesus wanted them to trust His word and not be frightened by any storms.

Sometimes we encounter great storms. We wonder why Jesus didn't warn us of the storm that was ahead of us. In John 16:33 Jesus told us, *"In the world you will have tribulation but take courage; I have overcome the world."* That is all the warning we need, and also all the assurance we need. Troubles will come, but we need not fear them. In this world we will encounter storms but Jesus is greater than the storms. In Him we will overcome them. Jesus wants us focused on His promises and not to be alarmed by troubling situations that come our way. Jesus didn't tell the disciples about the storm because they didn't need to know. It wouldn't change anything. They would get to the other side and meet Jesus, just as He said.

Our hearts need to be settled on God's Word and promises. Our eyes need to be alert to Jesus coming to us in the storm. Unless our hearts are settled on His word, and our eyes expectant and vigilant, we may miss Jesus when He comes to us in the storm. One of the worst mistakes we can make as Christians is to gaze upon our circumstances instead of upon the faithfulness of our God. Often we are like Peter in this story. Jesus beckoned him to come to Him. When he focused on Jesus, he walked on the water despite the storm. When he took his eyes off Jesus, and focused on the wind and the waves, he became afraid and started to sink (Matt. 14:24-34).

Storms in life are inevitable, even though unwelcome. Before things can change God must allow disruption to our status quo. Before something new can be born there must be birth pangs to shift things and prepare a body for birth. In 1984, I was on staff at a church overseeing college and high school ministry. All of my focus, vision and dreams were for that ministry and its students. But then came a great storm and upheaval. It came despite my efforts and was beyond my control. I was devastated and felt lost. God was preparing to promote me. But I was so focused on what I was losing that I could not see where He was taking me. God was calling me to start a church.

Jesus didn't send the disciples into that sea to drown, but to cross over to a new shore where He would meet them. We have to let go of the safe and comfortable if we are to receive something new. Often we only let go when we are in the middle of a storm. God doesn't want us to have our eyes looking back to the shore we are leaving, or the storm we find ourselves in, but on the shore where He is taking us.

After the storm stopped, they had a deeper faith and a greater appreciation for Jesus. They said, *"You are certainly God's Son"* (Matt. 14:33). God intends us to come through our storms with greater faith and trust in Jesus. You may be going through a storm; you may feel lost and confused, but Jesus will take you through it to another shore.

Prayer - Help me trust You when I am in a storm. Help me remember Your ways and rest in Your promises so I will have eyes to see You walking on the water and coming to me. Help me to keep my eyes on the shore You're taking me to and not the shore I had to leave or the storm I'm in.

The Blessings of Honor

"...for those who honor Me I will honor and those who despise me shall be lightly esteemed." I Samuel 2:30

What is honor? And what does it mean to honor God? Honor is one of the great secrets to life. Understanding and practicing honor changes people's lives. The Hebrew word translated as honor here is *"Kabod"* which literally means, "to make heavy"- that is to give weight to. God says if we honor Him, He will honor us. On the other hand, if we despise Him, He will esteem us lightly. To despise does not mean to hate. In some ways its worse. It means to "treat lightly, take for granted, to ignore or forget." God says that if we regard Him that way (and many do), then His regard and care for us will be proportional. Failure to show honor to God is the root of so many other sins and the pathway to deception and suffering (Rom. 1:21).

The honor that we show God is different than the honor that He shows us. Ours is the honor shown by a lesser to a greater Being. We honor Him we when show Him gratitude, pay careful attention to His words, obey Him, seek to please Him and declare His praise. As the Greater One, He honors us by recognizing us, revealing Himself to us, enriching us, empowering us, sharing His wisdom with us and promoting us. God says that if you will honor Me in the way you should, as a created being, I will honor you in the way that only I can as Creator of the Universe. How wonderful is that!

God's honor, blessings, care and provision generally don't come to us directly, but rather through channels and chosen instruments. For instance, God provides for a young child through her parents, supplies our needs through an employer, gives us protection through police and guides and counsels us through pastors and spiritual leaders. Therefore, God requires that we not only honor Him as the Source of all our blessings (James 1:17), but that we also honor the instruments He uses to bless us. We must awaken to the fact that, just as we are surrounded every day with opportunities to serve Jesus by serving those around us, so also we can show God honor by honoring those He uses to bless us (I Peter 2:13; I Tim. 5:17). The channel or instrument through which God's blessing comes represents the Source of the blessing. *If you dishonor the instrument, you dishonor the Source, and you disinherit yourselves from the full blessing God wants to give you.*

This is most especially true concerning parents and children. Ask yourself, "How was God's gift of life given to me?" It came through your parents. No matter how flawed or imperfect they were, they were God's instrument to give you life. If not for them, you would not have the glorious opportunity to spend eternity in paradise, living in total happiness, in the very presence of God. Wow-what a gift! God gave the gift of life directly to Adam when He breathed into His nostrils the breath of life (Gen. 2:7). Ever since then, the gift has been passed down through human parents. In Luke 3, the genealogy of Jesus is given thru Joseph's line all the way back to Adam. The final verse of that genealogy reads, *"the son of Enosh, the son of Seth, the son of Adam, the son of God" (Luke 3:38).* The human chain ends with Adam because Adam received his life directly from God. Your father and mother are your connecting link in a chain that stretches back to God. When we fail to honor a parent, then we fail to honor God because He is the Head of that chain and, therefore, the chain is holy.

That is why the first commandment dealing with human interaction, the 5th commandment tells us to honor our parents. It doesn't say to only honor the honorable ones. It says to honor them because the chain is holy. God says that if we keep that command, we will be blessed in the land (Ex. 20:12). Even if a parent was dishonorable, you should honor them for **your** sake, so you can receive God's blessing. Failure to honor our parents can invite great sorrows (Prov. 15:20; Prov. 30:17; Deut. 27:16). My father never allowed me to speak disrespectfully to my mother nor did I allow my children to. If you love your children, you will teach them to show you and your spouse respect.

God sends leaders, teachers, mentors and officials into our life with a benefit or blessing for us. When we honor that leader, we open up the package and get the reward (Matt. 10: 40-41). If we dishonor and reject them, we leave the package unopened and don't get the reward (Luke 19:16). We are called to show honor, not only to God and our leaders, but also to each other, *"Be devoted to one another in brotherly love; give preference to one another in honor"* (Rom. 12:10). We should try to outdo each other in showing one another honor. God's blessings truly flow when we create a culture of honor in our churches and families. Remember, honor flows both ways. When we honor God, He honors us. Honoring God truly is the key to life.

Prayer - Thank You for Your many blessings to me. Help me to be truly grateful for them and to honor You as I ought. I will endeavor to please You by giving reverence to Your word and obeying You. Help me to recognize and truly honor the agents and instruments You appoint for me. Help me to honor my family, church and all people.

Being Resilient

"I have told you these things, so that in Me you might have peace. In this world you will have trouble. But take heart! I have overcome the world." John 16:33 NIV

In 1965, Bill Bright of Campus Crusade published a small tract entitled, "The 4 Spiritual Laws," to help people share their faith. By 2006, it had been published in 200 languages and 2.5 billion copies had been distributed at which point they stopped counting. It has indeed been successful in helping people share their faith, but it was so popular that it also helped to create an imbalance in how many understand the Christian life. You may remember that the first law was, *"God loves you and has a wonderful plan for your life."* Now something profound changes in the mind of the believer when we substitute Bill Bright's words *"God loves you and has a wonderful plan for your life,"* for Jesus word's *"In this world you will have trouble. But take heart! I have overcome the world."* This switch puts our focus on the circumstances of this life instead of our spiritual walk with Jesus. Our feelings and responses become determined by our circumstances. After all, hasn't God promised that I would have a *"wonderful"* life?

Bill Bright merely meant to enable Christians to open up a spiritual conversation with a lost person. Yet the theology and expectations of many Christians have been more shaped by his words than by the words of Jesus. Many Christians have unrealistic expectations of this life. They expect continual happiness and a largely trouble-free life where they are treated fairly. It is heartbreaking to see Christians become so shaken in their faith when they encounter real trials and sorrows. Jesus didn't promise us an easy life. He promised something much better. He promised us a life of overcoming fellowship with Him. He said we should prepare ourselves for difficulties, opposition and even sorrows, but that, in Him, we could find peace, comfort, and strength to overcome. Knowing this makes us resilient.

For the Christian, the goal in this life is not pursuing ease and pleasure, it is pursuing obedience and fruitfulness. It's a great mistake to ground our hopes for happiness in the circumstances of this life. If we do, we may well wind up disappointed and disillusioned. But when we pursue obedience and fruitfulness we enter into God's joy and fellowship. Remember we were not created to pursue our own happiness but rather to *"enter into the joy of your Master"* (Matt. 25:23). God's joy is far, far better and more lasting than fleeting happiness.

People fear facing suffering and troubles because they don't yet understand the faithfulness of God's grace in time of need. God promises us, *"And as your days, so shall your strength be"* (Deut. 33:25 NKJV). God's strength to you will be equal to the challenges you face. Some people watch others go through great trials and think, "I could never endure that." That is because you can never understand the depths of God's grace available until you need it. Be assured of this. In whatever crisis you find yourself, God will give you the strength, comfort and peace to overcome it. Nor should we fear persecution and mistreatment. The truth is that Christians through all ages have faced persecution (II Tim. 3:12). In facing mistreatment for Jesus, we enter into *"the fellowship of His suffering"* (Phil. 3:10) wherein *"you are blessed because the Spirit of glory and of God rests on you"* (I Peter 4:14). Rather than fearing possible mistreatment we should thank God for His Presence, blessing and help in the midst of it. We should also thank Him that, compared to the great majority of Christians who have ever lived, ours is so light.

There is something wrong with the teaching in many of our churches today if it is not preparing Christians to face and overcome life as it is. It's wrong to only pray that we be spared trials, tests and difficulties. We should also pray for strength, grace, joy and fruitfulness if they come. Remember that our Master, Jesus, was described as *"a Man of sorrows and acquainted with grief"* (Is. 53:3). Just as He overcame them, so shall we.

Jesus didn't promise us a trouble-free life. He promised us His overcoming Presence and help in this life and great rewards in the next. Many Christians are so fixated on the blessings and pleasures of this life that they almost forget about the pleasures and rewards of the next. This world's troubles pass quickly and its pleasures are fleeting. But the rewards in the next are forever and ever and ever. Whatever the future holds, remember Jesus' words, *"Do not let your heart be troubled; believe in God, believe also in Me"* (John 14:1). Such simple faith will prepare you for whatever the future brings.

Prayer - Help me to keep my mind stayed on You rather than on the changing affairs of this world. I commit to live in Your joy rather than try to pursue mere happiness. I choose obedience and fellowship with You over the fleeting pleasures of this world. I thank You for the strength, comfort and peace that allows me to overcome any challenge or hardship I may face.

The Greatest Gift

"And when they heard this, they quieted down and glorified God, saying, 'Well then, God has granted to the Gentiles also THE REPENTENCE THAT LEADS TO LIFE.'" Acts 11:8

Most people have a negative understanding of repentance and so tend to avoid any talk of it. However, repentance is a precious gift that leads to freedom, truth and life. True repentance yields incredible blessing and increase. Repentance is positive and not negative. The Bible teaches that repentance is a turning toward God - the Source of truth, love and joy, *"... that they should repent and turn to God"* (Acts 26:20). One of the words translated as "repent" is the Greek word *epistrepho* which comes from two Greek words meaning "to turn" and "towards." Repentance is turning towards God. Of course, turning to God, by definition, means a turning away from ungodliness, deception, and sin.

Depression does not come from repentance but from the failure to repent. Heaviness is the spirit of turning away from God, not of turning to Him. Repentance brings an increase to your life, not a subtraction. It expands your personality and freedom, rather than diminishing them, because it adds the grace and blessing of God. Inevitably, when a person truly repents in some area, they experience great joy and victory. On the other hand, it is those who resist the influence of God's Spirit and fail to repent that become miserable.

Why is repentance so indispensable? The answer is found in understanding our fallen human nature. Due to the effect of sin separating us from God, we find our natural self fatally flawed. We were created to love and worship the One who created us. However, cut off from our Creator, we instead come to love, worship and serve ourselves. We were created to live in a dependent and secure relationship with God. However, separated from Him by sin, we find ourselves living lives of anxiety, fear and insecurity. We were created to overcome in His strength, however now we find ourselves weak, often defeated and overcome by addictions, deception and discouragement. This is reality and we won't make progress until we are willing to face the brutal truth. We are not enough in ourselves and we need God.

Through our initial repentance we come to Jesus as Savior, receive forgiveness and are born again to eternal life. However, repentance is not a one-time event. Rather it is an ongoing process or lifestyle in which we turn from the brokenness and limits of our fractured nature and receive from the perfect and limitless nature of God. A lifestyle of such repentance is at the heart of a victorious Christian life. The great reformer, Martin Luther, said that repentance was the daily fleeing from our brokenness to the wholeness of Christ. He called it "the happy exchange." It is a wonderful thing to exchange your weakness for His strength and your ignorance for His wisdom. In His perfect love and faithfulness, we find total love and security. Repentance is the key offered us that unlocks the door to the super-abundance of God's Kingdom. Jesus began His preaching with the words, "Repent, for the Kingdom of God is at hand" (Matt. 4:17).

Repentance means that we must not only turn from sin, but also from our self-centered nature and independence from God. The Bible says we must turn *"from dead works to serve the living God"* (Heb. 9:14). Dead works are any efforts that flow from our own strength and wisdom rather than Christ. They are called "dead" because they lack the life-giving power of God and cannot satisfy us. We may concoct arguments to rationalize when we do wrong or try to justify ourselves through doing good works or through achievement. We may try to comfort ourselves with drugs, alcohol, sex, pornography, internet addiction, or other mood-altering behaviors. Such dead works only result in distracting us and keeping us from experiencing the forgiveness, power and deliverance that only comes through repentance. We must turn not only from the things we are ashamed of but also the things we boast of and falsely trust in. If we continue to cling to these things after coming to Jesus, we will never know the freedom and victory that are ours in Christ alone.

Repentance and faith will take you to a better place. The main reason people keep clinging to dead works is because they don't believe God will give them a better future through repentance. Many try to escape the initial feelings of guilt and failure when God's Spirit begins stirring in them. But we must not hide from His light. *The darkness might feel safe but it is not our friend; it is the devil's torture chamber.* Only when we let God bring things into the light can we be healed and transformed. Do not hide from His conviction, rather let it do its complete work.

We must welcome God's gift of repentance, knowing that it leads to freedom, growth and joy. God's call to repentance is also an invitation to share in His riches and glory! God's conviction must not be taken lightly or resisted lest we become increasingly hard hearted. Remember, the same sun that softens wax hardens clay. *"Today, if you hear His voice, do not harden your hearts"* (Heb. 3:7-8).

Prayer - I ask You to illuminate my mind and cause me to understand Your gift of repentance so that I might come to embrace a lifestyle of repentance rather than resist it. In this way may the doorway to Your riches and blessings be fully opened to me.

Are You Angry With God?

"These things I have spoken to you, so that in Me you may have peace. In the world you have tribulation, but take courage; I have overcome the world." John 16:33

Have you ever felt let down by God? Have you ever felt that God didn't come through for you, or protect you, or provide for you? Perhaps it was when you were young. Many people carry wounds from their past. They may wonder where God was or why He didn't intervene. When we believe that God failed to properly care for us, an anger slowly settles in our heart, sometimes almost unnoticed.

Most believers understand we shouldn't be angry at God and that it is not in our best interest. So we try not to admit it, even to ourselves. But the symptoms are there for us to see. Many feel a spiritual dullness. For them worship often feels empty and they wonder why they don't get as much out of it as others. Sermons seem boring and personal devotions dry. Unresolved anger at God hardens our heart and makes us feel that God doesn't speak to us. And since we feel God failed us, we can't rest in His promises. This opens the door to many fears, worries and anxieties. And because a hardened heart has difficulty receiving the ministry of the Holy Spirit, we lack His joy, peace, hope and strength. As a result, we battle with discouragement, depression and fatigue.

Strained and broken relationships is another symptom. Our

fundamental relationship is to the One who created us and when anger diminishes that relationship, then all other relationships are affected. We project our distrust and disappointment with God into every other relationship. We have a hard time forgiving and trusting others. We guard ourselves, even from those who love us. People who suffer from having anger at God feel restless, discontented and fundamentally unblessed. Since they can't fully find rest and comfort in God, they and are tempted to find counterfeit rest and comfort in things like alcohol, applause and pornography.

Anger at God comes with a high price. So why be angry with Him? After all, did God not prove His perfect love for us by sending His own Son Jesus to die for us? The truth is, often our anger is rooted in a false expectation of what God has promised us. Many think God promises us a life free from suffering where God protects us from the hurtful actions of others. But God has not promised us that. Here is what Jesus promised us, *"I have told you all this so that you in Me you may have peace. In this world you will have trouble. But take heart I have overcome the world"* (John 16:33).

Jesus didn't promise that people would treat us fairly or that we would be spared suffering. He told us we would have troubles in this broken world. What He promised us is His help, comfort and overcoming power in the midst of mistreatment and difficulties. Remember, Jesus is our pattern and He experienced rejection, betrayal, physical abuse and suffering. Yet He overcame them all and now sits at the right hand of the Father. He promises us the same overcoming life. He promises that He can bring us good out of even the worst situations (Rom. 8:28).

If we surrender our unmet false expectations that embitter us, then we can experience His peace, joy, comfort, empowerment and blessings. The truth is, we can't accuse God of unfaithfulness and receive from Him at same time. The finger pointed at God in accusation is different than the open hand that receives from God. We can't accuse God of unfaithfulness in the past and believe in His faithfulness for today or the future. God doesn't promise to answer all of our questions, but He promises us His grace and help in all our present struggles.

When you are suffering, asking "why" is the wrong question. Often looking back from a future vantage point, we will understand the "why." But for now, the proper questions are "how" and "what." That is, "how" can I glorify God in this situation? After all, that is our God given purpose, and in doing it we find joy, fulfilment and experience the Lord's pleasure. The second question is "what?" What resources and grace has God set aside for me so that I can overcome and be victorious over this situation?

The worst mistake we can ever make is to have anger or doubt against the One who loves us with so perfect a love that He had His Son suffer on a cross for us. Satan's goal is to get us to doubt God's love and fill us with anger, pain and despair so that we are driven to sinful and self-destructive activities. Our responsibility is to trust God, believe in Him and fight the devil's lies.

Prayer - Father forgive me for sometimes doubting Your love in the midst of suffering and disappointment, and then holding secret anger towards You in my heart. Thank You for Your constant faithfulness. Help me to trust in Your promises at all times.

Day 29

Being Salt and Light

"You are the salt of the earth; but if the salt has become tasteless, how can it be made salty again? It is no longer good for anything, except to be thrown out and trampled underfoot by men. You are the light of the world. A city set on a hill cannot be hidden." Matthew 5:13-14, 16

Jesus makes two important points about His people. You and I are the salt of the earth and the light of the world. Salt to us is mostly a seasoning but in the time of Jesus it had even more important uses. It was highly valued for its healing and preserving qualities. It was the world's first antibiotic because it is very effective in killing bacteria. Even today we gargle with it to fight sore throats and rinse our mouths with it to heal mouth sores. But perhaps even more importantly it was the world's preservative. Before refrigeration, it was rubbed into meat and vegetables to preserve them. Therefore, salt was of extreme value. Roman soldiers were sometimes paid with it. In fact, our word *"salary"* is derived from the Latin word for salt. In calling us "salt" Jesus is pointing out not only our role but also the spiritual power He has given us. We have been given the power to overcome the corruption of the society around us and bring healing into lives, marriages, families, neighborhoods and cities.

But salt has to be applied to the site of the infection or be rubbed into the meat if it is to work. If salt merely sits in isolated salt piles, it does no good. So Jesus sends us out into the world. The Pharisees of Jesus' time held themselves aloof from those who were not as "righteous" as they believed themselves to be. But Jesus was different. In fact,

He was criticized for being *"a friend of tax collectors and sinners"* (Luke 7:34). He went into their homes and sat and listened to them, so He could understand them and speak to their situation. Jesus said that He was like a doctor who is called to go to those who are not well (Mark 2:17). He calls us to do likewise. Something profound happens when we enter into the world of lost people with understanding and love. People open their hearts to us and we can bring healing. But Jesus points out that we must retain our "saltiness"- that is we must live as genuine, faithful and life-giving disciples. If we get absorbed into the world's ways or turn our back on a hurting world, we lose the Spirit's power to heal and preserve and are instead mocked and ridiculed.

Jesus also said that we were the "light of the world." Notice He didn't say we were *like light*, as if merely drawing an analogy. He said we *were light*. In other words, we have the same properties in the spiritual world that light has in the physical world. Think of how this is true. Darkness is merely the absence of light. Darkness only exists where light does not shine. When you turn your lights off in your house, darkness rushes in to fill it but when you turn them back on, the darkness recedes. So it is in the spiritual. We must let our light penetrate into the darkness and shine in the midst of it. To the extent that you and I let our light shine in our family, neighborhood, city or nation, the darkness will recede.

Think about it. All living things are naturally drawn towards light. Plants and vines bend and grow towards sunlight. Jesus said, *"I am the Light of the world"* (John 8:12). He is the spiritual Light Source that all life seeks and is drawn to. That's why Jesus could say, *"And I, if I am lifted up from the earth, will draw all men to Myself"* (John 12:32). Ever since Jesus' crucifixion His Spirit can enter any heart and draw them, if only we will lift Jesus up before their eyes by proclaiming

Him. When you humbly converse with sinners, you will find that Jesus has already been at work in their life, drawing them to Himself and His truth. That is why it is so important that we be good listeners, so we can hear where Jesus has been at work in them and build upon it.

Everything that is good and true in a person is drawn to the Light of Christ, but everything that is shameful and deceitful hides from that Light. This creates a tug of war inside people. Think what this means for your own soul. If you honestly open up your entire heart to the Light of Christ and the truth of His Word, then darkness, depression, deception and anger will flee before His light. But when we harbor secret sin or hide inner wounds and leave them in the dark, we won't be healed or grow. That is why it is so important that we don't justify our sins or hide our hurts but confess them and bring them into the light so God can forgive and heal them.

What an awesome responsibility and privilege it is to reflect Christ's Light to others. He is the Light but He shines through us. And just as white light is made up of seven different colors, so the light of Christ shines brightest in the church which is made up of people with different spiritual gifts and callings. Jesus said, *"Let your light shine before men that they might see..."* Some places are very dark and we must be willing to shine brightly so people can come to the Light and see. Wherever you find yourself, Christ can shine through you. Remember the song we sang in Sunday school as children- *"This little light of mine-I'm going to let it shine."*

Prayer - Thank You for saving me and preserving and illuminating my life. I rejoice that I now have the Light of Life in me. Send me wherever You want me to shine and empower me with Your Spirit to shine brightly so that people will come to You.

Day 30

Getting Your Harvest

"Do not be deceived, God is not mocked; for whatever a man sows, this he will also reap." Galatians 6:7

The last 9 words of the above passage spell out one of the most powerful and all-encompassing principles of life, the Principle of Sowing and Reaping. As I have counseled, pastored and watched thousands of people for more than 40 years, I have come to see that this principle is at the core of how life works. No other single factor even comes close in shaping a person's life or circumstances. Many people live in denial of this truth and try to gain good results and happiness from bad and immoral actions. Therefore, this principal comes with a special warning, *"Do not be deceived, God is not mocked."* It is a powerful deception indeed that leads us to try and rewrite reality and mock God by ignoring the Creator's Law. He spoke this inviolable law into existence on the third day of creation when He created plants and fruit trees on the earth with seed in them bearing fruit *"after their kind"* (Gen. 1:11). God gave creation the incredible power to multiply and increase but He put a limit on that power. Everything that reproduces can only reproduce after its own nature.

This law is true not only in agriculture and biology but in everything God created including the spiritual, moral and social realms. You can't create good by evil means. You can't create happiness for yourself by lying and cheating. You will only produce conflict and sorrow. This law works in every area of life; give a smile and you will get a smile, show respect to others and they will show you respect. Jesus said that if we would not judge and condemn others but rather be forgiving, that we would not be judged or condemned, and if we gave to others we would receive back with increase (Luke 6:37-38).

But if we are to gain a harvest, we must plant seeds. We can plant seeds confident that God will cause the growth (1 Cor. 3:7). If through fear, passivity or laziness we do not plant seeds, then we cannot get a harvest. The secret is to be proactive and always plant good seeds. We must learn to act rather than react. If we react to the evil that others do to us and respond in kind, then we are letting them determine what seeds we plant and therefore what harvest we will reap. Jesus taught His followers not to react to what others do but to instead plant good seed, *"... love your enemies, do good to those who hate you, bless those who curse you.... treat others the same way you want them to treat you"* (Luke 6:27-31). What a powerful and life-giving principle! In this way we overcome evil with good and inherit a blessed life. But remember that a farmer must be patient because after planting seeds, he must wait for the harvest. If a farmer plants on Monday and gets his harvest on Tuesday, that would be a miracle rather than "sowing and reaping." We too must be patient because there is often a growing season before the harvest comes. Many people give up on their harvest before its time has come.

Jesus teaches us that sowing seeds involves a mystery, *"and he goes to bed at night and gets up by day, and the seed sprouts and grows-how, he does not know. The soil produces crops by itself; first the blade, then the head, then the mature grain in the head. But* when the crop permits, he immediately puts in the sickle, because the harvest has come" (Mark 4:27-29). When seeds are placed in the ground, we can't see their progress. We must believe that God has placed life in that seed and that it will produce according to its DNA. Good seeds will produce a good harvest. We don't have to understand how it will happen. In its early stages it may not look like what we are hoping for. The tiny blade that first appear doesn't look like the stalks full of corn we are hoping for. When I was a little boy, I planted a vegetable garden but I began to pull up the little blades I thought were weeds not recognizing it was the beginning of my harvest. We must continue to water and wait in faith believing that God will bring forth a good harvest, despite how things may look, because we planted good seeds.

The Bible tells us that God supplies us with both "...*seed for the sower and bread for food*" (II Cor. 9:10). A farmer doesn't turn all of his harvest into bread but he uses some of it to plant for the next season. That which we make into bread is eaten and is gone. The potential for multiplication is only in the seed that we sow. This verse tells us that even when we think we only have a little, we must recognize that God has given us enough, so we always have something to sow. When you look at what the Lord has given you, how do you know which part of it is for bread and which part of it is seed to sow? Well, that depends on you. It all looks the same until you decide which is for seed and give it away. God wants to multiply what you have so you can be assured that if you sow some of it as seed, it will return to you "*pressed down, shaken together and overflowing into your lap*" (Luke 6:38). This means that the surest way to escape poverty and lack is to become a giver. I have learned that when I suffer lack it is the best time to give. Remember, "He who sows sparingly will also reap sparingly and he who sows bountifully will also reap bountifully" (II Cor. 9:6). Ask God where He wants you to sow some seed. And remember that sowing and reaping work in every area of life.

Prayer - Thank You for the principle of sowing and reaping. Thank You that I never have to be the victim of how others treat me but that I have the power to determine my harvest. Show me where to sow seeds as I trust You to cause the growth. Give me the faith to trust in Your promise despite the circumstances.

Enter His Rest

"Come to Me, all who are weary and heavy-laden, and I will give you rest. Take My yoke upon you and learn from Me, for I am gentle and humble in heart, and YOU WILL FIND REST FOR YOUR SOULS. For My yoke is easy and My burden is light."
Matthew 11:28-30

Jesus makes a wonderful promise here to give us rest. Many today are not at rest. People often tell me of all the stress they are under. Some feel like they are going pedal to the metal every day and the rpms are nearing redline. Rest means that you are no longer under that weight. If you have been on your feet all day, you are looking for someplace to sit down. When you stand, your legs bear your weight, but when you sit in a chair, your weight rests on something else. We say, "Sit down and take a load off your feet." This is the rest Jesus offers. The strain on our life is gone because Someone else is carrying the burden and weight. Jesus's rest is a very real and wonderful thing.

Unfortunately, many Christians have not fully entered His rest even though Jesus said that His rest is offered to *"all."* In order to enter His rest fully Jesus says that we must do two things. First, we must, *"take My yoke upon you."* A yoke is the harness that attaches oxen to their cart or load. To live in Jesus' rest, we must exchange our yoke for His. In other words, He will pull our heavy load if we will submit to His yoke, and His yoke is easy and His burden is light. Jesus says, *"If you will concern yourself with my business, I will concern Myself with yours."* If we are harnessed to our selfish ambition, sinful desires, past hurts, worries, fears and self-righteousness, we will never have rest. But if we yield to Jesus' Spirit and teachings, we will be free and know His rest. Jesus' second requirement to enter His rest is *"learn from Me."* We must understand life through His teaching. We must see things through His eyes, and follow in His steps. We can only enter His rest by becoming a disciple and learner of Jesus.

What an incredible, liberating and revolutionary concept to think of religion as rest, as something refreshing and invigorating. Through most of history religion has been viewed as burdensome duties and painful sacrifices all done to placate the gods. This is how the natural mind thinks, *"I have to do hard things I don't want to do in order to please God so He won't be mad at me and He will bless me."* This is how the Devil wants you to think about God. Without going into detail, the religions of the world are built upon this misunderstanding. Many people in America have this view as well. It's why I put off becoming a Christian, because I thought it would be too hard for me and I would fail. But Christianity is not like this. It is not burdensome but life giving. Even the Old Testament Priest had to wear linen robes rather than wool because linen breathes and God did not want His priests to sweat, because serving Him is not toilsome and burdensome. God wants our service to Him to be joyous and life-giving because He is our strength.

Unlike what I used to think before I was saved, Christianity is not a list of dos and don'ts we must first fulfill. Rather Christianity begins with a "BIG DONE." Jesus won salvation for us, once for all, on the cross and offers it to us as a free gift! Do you know what the easiest thing I ever did in my life was? It was getting saved! I didn't have to do anything accept admit I needed a Savior and Jesus came and filled my heart with His power and love. I didn't have to do a great deed or master difficult religious practices and techniques. As soon as I

97

admitted I needed a Savior I was saved and introduced to God as my Father. One moment I was oppressed, confused, anxious, guilt ridden and bound by alcohol and the next I was free and had peace and joy in my heart. It was all undeserved and unearned. That is Christianity! Christianity is not a burden; it is a liberating power. Resting in Jesus gives you His Power to overcome in everything, "*I can do all things through Him who strengthen me*" (Phil. 4:13).

Think of the wonderful rest Jesus gives us. He gives us rest from fear, anxiety and worry about the affairs of this life. What a heavy burden that is to carry. But Jesus said that if we would seek first God's Kingdom, He promises that every earthly need would be supplied to us (Matt. 6:31-33). He gives us rest from financial pressure, if only we enter into His abundant economy by tithing and giving (Malachi 3:10; Luke 6:38; Ps. 127:2). God gives us rest from religious striving, as well as the exhausting striving for identity and worth, by accepting us as His sons and daughters. What a great rest it is to experience God as our unfailing supply!

People work so hard trying to earn things that we can only receive as gifts such as love, acceptance, forgiveness, security and peace. Pursuing popularity, getting a promotion, getting a bigger house, taking another drink or eating another Big Mac won't fill up the emptiness or take away our pain, or make us feel worthwhile, loved and secure, or give us peace. But resting in Jesus will. Jesus says to us, "*Come to Me and I will give you rest.*" How wonderful that rest is!

Prayer - I want to enter and live in Your rest every day. I want to be taught by You and follow in all Your ways. I will focus on your concern and agenda and I will yield all of my concerns and needs into your faithful hands. I trust and rest in You.

Tuning Into God's Frequency

"But like the Holy One who called you, be holy yourselves also in all your behavior; because it is written, 'YOU SHALL BE HOLY, FOR I AM HOLY.'" I Peter 1:15-16

God defines Himself as holy, and He wants us to be defined by that term as well. We know that *"God is love"* because the Bible tells us so in 1 John 4:16. But did you know it is the only verse in the Bible that makes that statement (Go ahead and look it up). But the phrase *"God is Holy"* is in dozens of verses. God specifically states *"I am Holy"* 5 times (as in our passage) and His Spirit is specially referred to as the "Holy Spirit." Now why does the Bible state dozens of times that God is holy and only once that God is love? Perhaps it's because we are so quick to accept that God is love and so resistant to the idea that He is holy. God has many attributes but none more important than His holiness. It is continually sung and shouted in His Presence in Heaven by the Angels, *"…and day and night they do not cease to say, 'Holy, Holy, Holy is the Lord God, the Almighty, Who was and Who is and Who is to come'"* (Rev. 4:8 and see Isaiah 6:3).

In the Bible the Hebrew and Greek words translated as holy mean, *"pure…set apart…elevated…different from other things…devoted to God."* One way to think about it is that holiness is *that which is compatible with God's nature and environment* and sin or sinfulness is *that which cannot remain in God's Presence.* So God says in our passage, *"Be Holy for I am Holy."* The Bible says, *"Strive* for …. *holiness without which no one will see the Lord"* (Heb. 12:14 ESV). In other words, we will not be able to see or perceive God in this life or the next without pursuing holiness. We can't fellowship with an FM God if we are living on an AM frequency. Holiness is God's frequency. Holiness makes us compatible with God and sensitive to Him. God says, "If you want to know Me, get on My wavelength." The goal of every true Christian, who sincerely wants to know God, must be to pursue holiness.

Now we must understand that there are two dimensions to holiness. The first is *imputed* or *positional* holiness which is our being made objectively holy because we are forgiven and set apart to God by the blood of Christ. The second is *progressive* or *ethical* holiness which is being gradually transformed more and more into Christ's image and into godly thinking and behavior. The first kind is a gift and the second a calling. When God commands us to *"Be holy,"* or *"Strive for holiness,"* He is speaking of the second kind.

How important is holiness to God? How important should it be to you and me? Consider this, the words "holy" and "holiness" occurs 685 times in the NASB translation of the Bible, 186 of those in the NT. If you include the related words, "sanctify" and "consecrate" you get a total of 862 occurrences. Now compare that to other important words in the Bible. The word "love" in its various forms occurs 560 times and the words "faith" and "believe" occur 862 times. When we preach that God is love and requires that we love but not that He is holy and requires that we be holy, we are creating a false image of God. We are misrepresenting Him.

When we are saved, God places His Holy Spirit in us. His Spirit within us yearns that we live holy, that God's character be formed in us, and that we live on His frequency so we can fellowship with Him. In fact, the desire to pursue holiness is a necessary sign and proof that we have been born again by His Spirit. A primary motive in all of His dealings with us is that we may come to share in and reflect His holiness, *"He disciplines us for our good, so that we may share in His holiness"* (Heb. 12:10a). Holiness means pursuing God with all your heart, mind and strength. Holiness is thinking like God thinks and esteeming things according to His values. It is loving what God loves and turning away from what God hates (injustice, deception, hypocrisy, cruelty, gossip, lies, immorality, etc.). Therefore, a true Christian does not enjoy or join in with the ungodly philosophies, fads, or entertainments of the world, but is grieved by them. They desire God's approval over that of anyone else and so do not compromise but have the God-given courage to discriminate between right and wrong, even if it brings harsh criticism. Holiness is loving Christ enough to be willing to say no to wrong desires and appetites. Above all, holiness means desiring to be like Christ above that of any other desire.

Holiness is more than trying to subtract sin from your life, because holiness is an addition, not a subtraction. It is being filled with God's Presence - the Source of holiness. It is the replacement of that which is low and inferior with those things that are higher, nobler and more fulfilling. It is the replacement of fear, lust, strife and insecurity with love, joy, kindness and faith. True holiness is the opposite of being judgmental or "holier than thou" because holiness begins with an awareness of our own shortcoming before God. True holiness always sees others through God's eyes of compassion and love. Holiness brings the strength and beauty of God into our life. If we lose sight of the fact that God is holy, it will lead to a low view of God and therefore to a low way of living, but when we see God high and lifted up it elevates how we live. God invites you to share in His holiness.

Prayer - Thank You for making me holy through Christ. Thank You for Your Holy Spirit working in me so I can live holy and become Christ-like because that is my deepest desire. I want to live in fellowship with You and reflect Your goodness and holiness to the world.

Day 33

Live From the Inside Out

*"Watch over your heart with all diligence, for from it
flow the springs of life."* Proverbs 4:23

Our culture focuses on the outside, on a person's looks, clothes, car, home, possessions and titles. But as the above verse reveals, our life flows from the inside out and not the outside in. It is our character, attitude, beliefs and morals that will determine the quality of our life, not our possessions, circumstances or luck. We are encouraged to perfect our bodies, enhance our beauty and upgrade our homes and cars. But all the while something far more important to your future happiness and success is taking place inside of you. Your soul is being shaped and formed. Every day we see people walk around with beautiful bodies and huge muscles but inside their soul or inner man may be shriveled and ugly. It is the condition of your heart that will determine your life. A person can quit their job, divorce their spouse and move to another city, but you cannot divorce or move away from yourself. We will always live out what we are inside. It will determine the choices we make and the outcome of our life.

That's why the Bible teaches that inner well-being must come before true outward success, *"Beloved, I pray that in all respects you may prosper and be in health, just as your soul prospers"* (III John 2). A godly prospering soul is the foundation for true outward blessing and lasting happiness. The real issue in life is not what we get, but who we become. Therefore, we are told to *"watch over your heart with all diligence,"* because every choice we make changes us a little inside. We make choices and then our choices make us. Ultimately there are only two basic prototypes to conform our soul to and each choice makes us more like one or the other. The first is Jesus Christ who perfectly walked out God's will and the other is Satan, the original rebel. Jesus told some Pharisees that they were *"of your father the devil"*- *"the father of all lies"* (John 8:44). He said this because they agreed with his thinking, believed his lies and embraced his values.

The Bible tells us that physical discipline and exercise is good, but has only limited value compared to spiritual discipline which holds *"promise for the present life and also for the life to come"* (1 Tim. 4:8). People seldom fail due to a lack of physical strength but often fail due to a lack of spiritual and moral strength. In the same way, the greatest beauty is that which is within (1 Peter 3:3-4).

Daniel in the Bible was destined for failure. He grew up in a corrupt culture, during wartime, in a city under siege. At a young age his city was burned and he was taken from his family and deported to Babylon where he was put in a pagan school surrounded by pagan influences. But Daniel didn't fail, instead he distinguished himself and prospered, *"Then Daniel became distinguished above all the other high officials and satraps, because an excellent spirit was in him"* (Daniel 6:3 ESV). Daniel proved that in any circumstance you can have an "excellent spirit" and distinguish yourself. This is because life is 10% what happens to you and 90% how you respond to it. Every born-again Christian has received the Spirit of Jesus. How can anyone have a more excellent spirit than this? Galatians 2:20 says, *"Christ lives in me."*

Therefore, if you want can have an excellent spirit, make growth in Christlikeness your highest priority. The Bible tells us to imitate Christ (I Cor. 11:1). Therefore, evaluate every situation with the question, "Is there an opportunity to become more Christ-like through this?" Next, commit to think and meditate on what is excellent, *"whatever is true, whatever is honorable, whatever is right, whatever is pure, whatever is lovely, whatever is of good repute, if there is any excellence and if anything is worthy of praise, dwell on these things"* (Phil. 4:8). You can't develop an excellent spirit unless you fill your mind and heart with excellent things. A mind given to secular entertainment, celebrity gossip, online games and endless sports trivia won't produce an excellent spirit. How much time do you give to Bible study, worship, fellowship and reading excellent books- especially biographies of great Christians?

Finally, elevate your motivation in everything you do. Colossians 3: 23-24 says, *"Whatever you do, do your work heartily, as for the Lord rather than men, knowing that from the Lord you will receive the reward of the inheritance. It is the Lord Christ whom you serve."* Every task, even the unwelcome ones and the ones that go unnoticed is an opportunity to serve Christ with excellence. Turn everything you do into an act of worship and an expression of love to Jesus. Instead of complaining, ask, "How can I make this better; how can I add value?" Everything changes when you change the question from, "What's in it for me?" to "How can I serve Christ and change more into His image?"

We live in a time of pessimism and self-centeredness, but like Caleb from the Old Testament, we can have *"a different spirit"* (Numbers 14:24). Ask, "Where can I start to be more excellent?" Begin by starting in small things, one responsibility and one relationship at a time. Remember our choices make our character and our character makes our life.

Prayer - Help me to watch over my own heart. Although the world prizes the outward, help me to value my inner life above all. Help me to meditate on the good and to seize every opportunity to serve Christ with excellence that I may grow in Christ-likeness.

Day 34

The Prayer of Jabez

Jabez was more honorable than his brothers, and his mother named him Jabez saying, "Because I bore him with pain." Now Jabez called on the God of Israel, saying, "Oh that You would bless me indeed and enlarge my border, and that Your hand might be with me, and that You would keep me from harm that it may not pain me!" And God granted him what he requested.
I Chronicles 4:9-10

Our passage comes from the Book of I Chronicles. Chronicles means records and the book contains many lists of names, especially genealogies. The first nine chapters are made up almost entirely of genealogies. In Chapter 4 the list of names is interrupted in order to comment on one of the names. What was it about Jabez that merits special attention?

His mother named him Jabez which in Hebrew means "with pain" or "with sorrow." Some non-biblical Jewish sources fill in the details regarding him. As the story goes, shortly before he was born his father died. Jabez was born fatherless to a grieving widowed mother. To make it worse, his greedy older brothers divided the estate before he was born so he wouldn't get a share. As he grew up, he soon realized that he had no father to protect him or prepare him for life. He also had no inheritance waiting for him, and he could expect no help from his brothers who had so cruelly cut him out of the family.

But we also read that Jabez was honorable. Jabez had been dealt a bad hand and he could've become bitter, sought revenge, become an outlaw, or drowned his sorrow in a bottle. But instead, Jabez made an honorable decision that set him apart and got him memorialized in the Bible as an example to us. What was that decision? We read that *"Jabez called on the God of Israel."* The Hebrew word translated *"called on"* is the word *"quar"* which literally means "to cry out." It was not a half- hearted religious prayer. He called out with His whole being and entrusted himself completely to God.

Jabez prayed for 4 things. He prayed for God's blessing, God's promotion, God's presence, and God's protection. Our passage ends, *"And God granted him what he requested."* God will grant these same 4 requests to us. But first we must "cry out"-that is we must entrust our life entirely into God's hands, with complete confidence in His goodness and faithfulness. Jabez looked at himself. He had never known his father; he had no inheritance and he was born into a family that had betrayed and mistreated him. Jabez called out to God in his distress and put his trust in Him.

What do you do with your problems, mistreatment and sorrows? Each of us, no matter our background or circumstances, can make the same choice Jabez did. However, we will never cry out like Jabez did until we are disillusioned with everything but God. As long as your hope is in your schemes, or in other people or in your luck changing, you won't cry out. Whatever your situation, if you cry out to God with all your heart, He will hear you. The prophet Jonah, due to his disobedience, found himself in the belly of a great fish. He cried out to God and was heard and delivered. Peter walked on water until his faith failed and He started to sink. He cried out to Jesus and was saved. I remember the night I cried out, "I've made a mess of my life. I surrender my life to you. Please save me." God has been faithful to me since that day. He will be faithful to anyone who puts their total trust in Jesus and cries out sincerely from their heart. Whenever you are in trouble, cry out to Jesus.

Prayer - Help me to trust completely in Your goodness and faithfulness. Teach me to cry out to You when I am in trouble rather than to trust in my own schemes. Help me to live honorably even when surrounded by dishonorable people.

Be True to Yourself

"As in water a face reflects the face, so the heart of a person reflects the person." Proverbs 27:19

Few people in the ancient world had mirrors. The best way to see what you looked like was to look into still water. The writer here is saying, just as water accurately reflects your face, so your heart reveals the person you are. In other words, "If you want to know what you look like, gaze into a mirror, and if you want to know who you are, look into your heart." The Bible says that our heart defines us and reveals who we really are.

Evolutionists say that we are merely animals driven and defined by various drives, urges and appetites. The Bible associates these appetites and drives with our belly, probably because the drive to eat is perhaps the most pressing and most familiar one. Philippians 3:18-19 says there are many people *"whose god is their belly"* (NIV) or *"whose god is their appetite"* (NASB). Sigmund Freud said that since we are animals, there is nothing more real than these drives and appetites, so it's unhealthy to "repress them."

Who is right, the Bible or the evolutionists? Are we, as the evolutionists say, defined by our belly or as the Bible says, by our heart? This is a very important question for all of us. I had a friend once who was a member of our church. He had been married about 15 years and had two children. He told me one day he was going to leave his wife and children and enter the homosexual lifestyle because "he had to be true to who he really was." He obviously agreed with the evolutionists that He was defined by his appetites. This is the Big Lie- that you are defined by your temptations and appetites even if you did not choose them. But the Bible's Big Truth is- you are defined by your choices and actions not your temptations or urges. In other words, you are defined by what you choose to do, not by what you are tempted to do. Your heart is where you hold your beliefs, values and convictions while your belly merely represents your appetites. The question for each of us to decide is which of these define us and which will we follow. Unfortunately for my friend, and his family, he believed the lie.

What a tragic mistake. Our heart is eternal; it is the center of our being and defines who we really are, while our belly, or sinful appetites, is merely temporary and will pass away. Evolution says that we are just biological beings whose most important drive is to reproduce, so sex is all important. But the Bible says that we are spiritual beings, made in the image of God whose greatest need is to know God and fellowship with Him. True freedom is not the freedom to indulge in sin. True freedom is the freedom to know God, be set free from sins power and become the person God can make you.

But what about those strong temptations to do wrong? Do they define us and disqualify us from being acceptable to God? In Hebrews 4:15 we read that Jesus understands our weaknesses because He was, "tempted in all things as we are, yet without sin." In other words, Jesus experienced temptation but chose not to give into it. Therefore we are not condemned or disqualified simply because we are tempted. Our temptations do not define us, but our choices do. If I have horrible temptations and yet do not act them out, then I am righteous and pleasing to God. We don't like ambiguity so we don't like being both a sinner and a saint at the same time. But that is what we are. We are a sinner in that we will always have to struggle against sin. But we are a saint in that we have been forgiven our sins by the blood of Christ and set apart and empowered by the Holy Spirit to overcome sin. We will not be free from temptation until Christ returns (or we die), but we can still be overcomers in this life.

If you are tempted to steal, but do not, then you are not a thief. If you are tempted by immorality but because of your love for Jesus you turn away from it, then you are not immoral. It is not your temptations that define you, but your choices. You are never a hypocrite for going against your feelings or even against a strong persistent temptation (like my friend faced). You are only a hypocrite if you go against your beliefs and commitments. A Christian is not someone who is perfect but rather someone who is motivated by their love for Jesus to resist sin by the power of the Holy Spirit. Every temptation is an opportunity to show our love for Jesus. The more broken a person is, the greater opportunity for God to demonstrate His mercy and power.

God says that we must consider ourselves "to be dead to sin but alive to God in Christ Jesus" (Rom. 6:11). That means we say to temptation, "I know that you are always there but you do not define me, and you will not master me." Martin Luther said of temptation, "I can't stop a bird from flying over my head, but I can stop it from building a nest in my hair." You can't control what temptations assail you but you can refuse to identify with them or act upon them. Always remember that as we follow Jesus' teaching and grow in our ability to walk in the Spirit, we will grow in freedom (John 8:31-32; Rom. 8:13; Gal. 5:16). Also remember that God has declared you holy and acceptable.

Prayer- Thank You for declaring me righteous and accepted through Christ's sacrifice. Encourage me by your Spirit so I don't grow discouraged in my battle against temptation and fill me with Your joy as I watch myself being transformed by Your Spirit.

Day 36

God's Compassion

And a leper came to Jesus, beseeching Him and falling on his knees before Him, and saying, "If You are willing, You can make me clean." Moved with compassion, Jesus stretched out His hand and touched him, and said to him, "I am willing; be cleansed." Mark 1:40-41

Why did Jesus heal the man in the above story? What motivated Him to act? The man didn't display great faith, he wasn't even sure Jesus wanted to heal him, he only believed that He could. Please notice it says that Jesus healed the man because He was "*moved with compassion.*" Eight times in the New Testament we read that Jesus acted because he was moved with compassion.

God is moved to act by His compassion. Compassion is a feeling of deep sympathy for another's suffering and a strong desire to help. God's compassion is all that's needed for Him to act. God feels compassion for people in their brokenness and need. God did not send Jesus to earth because we deserved it or because of Israel's great faith, but because of His compassion.

In Psalm 103:13-14 we read, "*Just as a father has compassion on his children, so the Lord has compassion on those who fear Him. For He Himself knows our frame; He is mindful that we are but dust.*" Now human fathers and mothers don't only have compassion on their children when they are doing well. We feel compassion for them even when they do bad and suffer for it. How much more patient is the Lord's compassion. He knows how imperfect we are. God wants us to live with great confidence and hope in the greatness of His compassion.

The prophet Jeremiah wrote, "*The Lord's loving kindnesses indeed never cease, for His compassions never fail. They are new every morning; Great is your faithfulness*" (Lamentations 3:22-23). Do you awaken every morning with a confidence in God's great compassion for you? Do you live out of an awareness of His kindness and faithfulness every day? They are new every morning. What is your first thought as you start out each day? Do you say, "Good morning, Lord" or do you say, "Good lord, it's morning again?" Do you feel discouraged and overwhelmed, or are you full of hope and joy? Trusting in the Lord's compassion and faithfulness will keep your head up.

God's compassion is one of the great realities of life. It's God's response to lostness, brokenness, and pain. Make no mistake, God judges sin and there are consequences for wrong doing, but it is always mixed with His compassion and a grace to repent.

God wants us to live each day secure in His compassion and extend that same compassion to others. He wants us to be His instruments of compassion to a dark and lost world. All around us are lost and hurting people in need. Many may look very different from you and may even act wickedly. It's easy to feel estranged and be critical of them. But when you see them through God's eyes of compassion, the world will never look the same. In fact, you won't be the same, because you change when you are an instrument of His compassion.

There is a big difference between being friendly and being a friend. Greeters at Walmart and baristas at Starbucks greet customers with a friendly smile. But people need more than that. They need someone to befriend them and enter into their world. Many people visit our churches and see friendly faces (just like at Walmart), but months later they still haven't found a friend. Our calling isn't just to be friendly but to truly befriend people. God's compassion moves us to act. If you put yourself between God's compassion and a person in need, you will see the Lord use you. Even if your hand is empty, if you will extend to someone in need, you will see God fill your hand with His mercy as it reaches them.

What you and I need today is a deep, enduring conviction regarding the Lord's great compassion. James 5:11 says, "*The Lord is full of compassion and mercy.*" God's compassion is one of the great but often forgotten realities of life. Knowing God's great compassion changes how we look at the world today. It is our hope and the hope for America.

Prayer - Thank You for Your great compassion. Help me to live each day confident that You feel compassion for me at all times. Help me to be Your instrument of compassion to others today.

Starting and Finishing

"And we desire that each one of you show the same diligence so as to realize the full assurance of hope until the end, so that you will not be sluggish, but imitators of those who through faith and patience inherit the promises." Hebrews 6:11-12

In the 1968 Olympics, Tanzanian marathon runner John Akhwari fell badly, injuring his shoulder and dislocating his knee. After receiving medical attention, he rose to his feet, and to the astonishment of everyone, began to hobble toward the finish line which was still miles ahead. He limped into the nearly empty Olympic Stadium for the final lap over an hour after the man who had won. With great difficulty he crossed the finish line. When asked why he didn't just quit when he was injured, he replied, "My country did not send me 7000 miles to begin a race, but to finish one."

It's fine to start something, but it doesn't mean much if you don't finish. It's been said that the two hardest things in life are starting and finishing. It's hard to start something; it's much easier to procrastinate, or even sit frozen – afraid to move forward. But it's even harder to finish. It is reported that 80% of all New Year's resolutions fail. Nearly 40% of incoming college freshman will drop out before they graduate, and nearly half of all first marriages end in divorce. Likewise, many start the Christian life with enthusiasm – but far fewer finish well. Many drop out altogether.

What about you? What are you willing to do to make sure you finish? You may have good intentions, but having good intentions is not enough. Every couple getting married starts out with good intentions for a lifelong relationship of respect, love, and happiness. But not all finish. Every person who starts out with Christ intends to live a life of honor and faithfulness to Him.

Almost all people start out with good intentions. What differentiates people is not so much their intentions but rather the priorities they set for themselves. Many fall into the trap of letting the demands of life, or the influence of others, cause them to prioritize secondary things and neglect the most important ones. Jesus warns us against doing this. In fact, He taught us that if we keep first things first, He would see that all secondary things will be *"added to us"* (Matt. 6:33).

Today's verses teach us two important secrets if we are to finish our race. First, it tells us that we must be diligent rather than sluggish (to be careless and procrastinate). Every activity in life can be done either sluggishly or diligently. Now, you can afford to be sluggish in some things, but not in others. It's really not that important if your car is dirty, your yard neglected, your Christmas cards don't go out on time, or your kids miss a practice. The consequences are not serious. But it is not so with other matters, such as your spiritual life, your marriage and raising your children. With these we must be diligent – we must be persistent with them and attend to them carefully, for these truly determine the trajectory and outcome of our lives. We dare not let other activities rob us of making the necessary investment in prayer and Bible reading, fellowship for ourselves and our children, or investing in our marriage, etc.

Life is filled with many demands. The truth is, we cannot do everything with excellence. We do not have sufficient time or strength. We must set priorities. If we are to succeed at the most important, we must be willing to risk failing at the lesser things. We must choose which things we are willing to fail at and which things we are not. You can't let others determine your priorities. If you always have to say yes to other people's expectations, then you will find yourself saying no to God's. This is challenging for us. It takes planning and discipline.

Second, we must imitate those who finish well. We must imitate *"those who through faith and patience inherit the* promises." Many in the Bible didn't finish well, such as King Saul, Judas and Demas (II Tim. 4:10). Others such as Elijah, Joseph, Daniel, Jesus and Paul did. I thank God for the many finishers I have known in my life. They inspire me. Who are you going to imitate? Do you have people in your life that can serve as models for you? If you want to be a finisher, then imitate them.

Stay faithful even in difficult times. Never forget that God is faithful and that He is your rewarder (Heb. 11:6). Only then will you reach the goal and finish well.

Prayer – I want to go beyond just having good intentions. I want to follow through and finish things well. Help me to prioritize my life according to Your value system and not the world's. Help me to be diligent in the areas that truly matter.

When Your Faith Is Tested

"Without becoming weak in faith, he contemplated his own body, now as good as dead since he was about a hundred years old, and the deadness of Sarah's womb; yet, with respect to the promise of God, he did not waver in unbelief but grew strong in faith, giving glory to God." Romans 4:19-20

Abraham faced a crisis of faith. God had given Him a clear word that He would have a child, born from His wife, Sarah, and that the child would be the first of a great multitude of descendants (Gen. 15:5 and Gen. 22:17). The promise to Abraham had first been given many years prior. All through the intervening years, Sarah had remained barren. And now He could see that both he and Sarah were seemingly beyond the years where giving birth was possible. He was faced with a choice. Would he believe what his eyes saw and his mind reasoned, or would he continue to believe God's Word?

All of us face crises of faith in our lives when the circumstances around us and our natural reasoning lead us to question God's promises to us. Perhaps you are facing one now. We interpret delays and disappointments in a way that cast doubt on what we believe. Like Abraham, we are being tested. The test is, will we succumb to and be defeated by our flawed reasoning, or will we surrender our thinking to God's Word - which is perfect? Abraham chose to believe God's promises above even his own perceptions. We read that, as a result, Abraham *"grew strong in faith, giving glory to God."*

In a crisis of faith, the issue isn't the faithfulness of God or the truth of His promises, for God cannot lie (Titus 1:2), nor can He be unfaithful (II Tim. 2:13). The real issue is our lack of understanding and the deficiency of our thinking. The key to blessedness is to live by faith in what God has said, rather than the carnal reasoning of our natural mind. To do so is not being irrational, it is being super-rational. It means that we go beyond the limits of our present understanding and draw instead upon God's perfect knowledge and understanding. Abraham did so and became the father of many nations.

This has always been the test that faces humanity. Adam and Eve lived in a perfect environment and yet they failed. God was faithful to supply them with everything they needed. But as we saw in a previous meditation, God placed two trees in the Garden of Eden. The Tree of the Knowledge of Good and Evil represented Adam and Eve choosing to decide good and evil for themselves, using their own reason and judgment. The second tree, the Tree of Life, represented living in union with and dependence upon God, being led by His truth and Spirit. Under Satan's influence, Eve looked at the Tree of Knowledge and reasoned in her mind. Her conclusion was different from God's Word, and so she ate the forbidden fruit. The result was not happiness and gain, but rather the loss of freedom and blessing.

This is the fundamental choice for each of us. Will I allow my emotions and reasoning to rule my life and rob me of God's blessings, or will I live trusting in God's perfect wisdom, power and love? The human mind is untrustworthy. We have limited understanding, we misinterpret things, and we even lie to ourselves. Therefore, I cannot rely upon my own understanding.

Proverbs 3:5 counsels us, *"Trust in the Lord with all your heart and do not lean on your own understanding."*

We become overcomers by choosing God's truth over our feelings and reasoning. Jesus showed us the way to victory. He did not follow His emotions, nor was He led by His physical senses or reasoning. The prophet Isaiah said of Him, *"The Spirit of the Lord will rest on Him, the spirit of wisdom and understanding... And He will delight in the fear of the Lord, and He will not judge by what His eyes see, nor make a decision by what His ears hear; but with righteousness He will judge..."* (Is. 11:2-4). In the same way, we have received the Spirit of God to give us wisdom and understanding. And we, too, should delight ourselves in the fear and reverence of the Lord and His Word.

Having a crisis of faith is difficult and painful. However, it is a necessary part of our spiritual development. It is necessary that we face delays, disappointments and contrary circumstances, because like Adam and Eve, we must be tested so that we learn to eat from the Tree of Life. Every test we face trains us to live by faith and trust in God rather than our human perspective. In this way we become mature and overcoming believers, fit for God's use (Heb. 5:14).

Prayer – Help me to be steadfast when my faith is being tested, secure in the conviction that Your promises are true and You are faithful. Let me not be shaken by my emotions or wild thoughts, but enable me to rest in Your promises. I want to be found faithful and gain the promises as Abraham did.

Worship God

"But an hour is coming, and now is, when the true worshipers will worship the Father in spirit and truth; for such people the Father seeks to be His worshipers. God is spirit, and those who worship Him must worship in spirit and truth." John 4:23-24

A Samaritan woman had asked Jesus where the proper place to worship God was. Jesus told her it was at the Temple in Jerusalem. Then He said something shocking. He said that the day was soon coming when the temple and its rituals would be abandoned for a new, more God pleasing kind of worship. It would be worship *"in spirit and truth for such people the Father seeks to be His worshipers."* What a life changing truth! God looks for and seeks out worshippers.

Many people struggle to connect with God. They say, "God seems so far away." But *Jesus says here that if you will worship God, He will find you!* What an amazing and powerful truth! This means that if I offer God true worship, He will find me and strengthen me with His presence. In any circumstance I can find God's presence and help because in any circumstance, no matter how bad, I can worship Him. Paul and Silas were arrested and beaten and thrown into prison in Philippi. But while in jail, they began to worship God and He came to them and delivered them (Acts 16: 23-26).

Jesus said there were two requirements for the worshipers God will seek. First, they must worship in spirit. For Jews of Jesus' time worship was primarily the outward rituals of the temple. But Jesus' coming changed everything. We have now been given the Holy Spirit so worship must come from within. True worship requires our spirit responding to God's Spirit, who inspires and guides our worship. We need the Holy Spirit to worship right!

Worship must also be in truth. True worshipers must have true biblical beliefs and live according to God's truth. We can't worship in spirit and truth if we are living a life that grieves the Holy Spirit. In Luke 6:46 Jesus asked, *"Why do you call Me, 'Lord, Lord,' and do not do what I say?"* Calling Jesus "Lord" is an act of worship. It is a contradiction to claim to worship One whom you won't obey. This is why some Christian's worship is empty. It is neither accepted nor embraced by God.

In every scene of God's Heavenly throne room in the Bible there are always two things present. First, He is seated on a throne because God is the absolute authority wherever He dwells. The second is that worship is always happening. Heaven is a place of worship. That is why when we worship with obedient hearts, we can bring heaven to earth! Everything has a natural habitat where it can be found - an environment that suits it and corresponds to its nature. God has an environment where He chooses to be found - one that is in keeping with Who He is. Psalm 22:3 (KJV) says that God *"inhabits the praises of Israel."* The NASB renders it *"You who are enthroned upon the praises of Israel."* Not only does God choose to dwell in our praises, He also rules and does mighty works where there is true worship! If we want to enter into His mighty presence, we must remember that Psalm 100:4 tells us to *"Enter His gates with thanksgiving and His courts with praise."*

So many in our culture have it backwards. We were not created to receive praise – but to give it. We were not made to esteem ourselves but to esteem Him. Self-esteem is self-love, self-devotion and self-worship. When we change the focus of our worship and esteem, we change the source we draw from. We begin to draw from an all-powerful and never-failing Source. Worship lifts us from self- consciousness to God consciousness. It elevates our vision from our own limitations to God's riches and from fear to faith. As creatures, we are never more fully human or alive than when we are worshipping our Creator. Worship is liberating, thrilling and empowering! You don't have to wait until you are at church to worship and praise, you can do it right now. Just begin by thanking and praising Him.

Prayer - Help me to live a holy life and to yield to Your Spirit so I can worship in spirit and truth. I want to esteem You rather than seeking to esteem myself. I want to know You as my never-failing Source. Give me a thankful and willing spirit so I can offer You constant praise and worship.

Growing Stages

"I am writing to you, little children, because your sins have been forgiven you for His name's sake. I am writing to you, fathers, because you know Him who has been from the beginning. I am writing to you, young men, because you have overcome the evil one. I have written to you, children, because you know the Father. I have written to you, fathers, because you know Him who has been from the beginning. I have written to you, young men, because you are strong, and the word of God abides in you, and you have overcome the evil one."
I John 2:12-14

This passage addresses three basic phases of Christian growth: little children, young men, and fathers. God's family, like all families, has members at different stages of life. These stages are not determined by age but by spiritual growth. All of us are at one of these three stages, or maybe you are in transition from one stage to the next. When you know what stage you are in, your life becomes more understandable and you can be prepared for what comes next. When we are in transition to the next stage, it can be very confusing if we don't understand what is happening. We get very comfortable in our present stage, but God is committed to moving us forward into maturity and the fullness of Christ.

The first stage is "little children." Two things mark this stage. First, their sins are forgiven (vs. 12). At the moment you receive Jesus as your Savior, your sins are forgiven as a free gift. Second, they know the Father (vs. 13). At the moment you receive Christ as Savior, you receive God's Spirit and are born again. Your spiritual eyes are opened and you are introduced to God as your Father and experience His love. Meeting our Heavenly Father is the most wonderful experience available in this life. Just like in the natural, when you are a spiritual "little child," everything is done to protect you, every need is quickly attended to and your cries and prayers receive an immediate response. Sometimes Christians wrongly refer to this stage as the honeymoon stage, but really it is the baby or "little child" phase. The key assignment in this stage is to bond with and learn to trust completely in your Heavenly Father's love and faithfulness. And like in the natural, this is carefree and joyous stage, but it is not a permanent one, and we can't remain in it forever.

The second stage is the young man or young women stage (vs. 13, 14). Just like in the natural, this stage is challenging but also exciting! It's the stage where we move from childishness to productivity. The good news is that it's a time when we discover God strength and become overcomers. The bad news is that we learn this strength by wrestling and overcoming temptation and the power of the enemy. This is when we learn to *"be strong in the Lord and the strength of His might"* (Eph. 6:10). We have to battle (and lose a few) so that we learn the Source of our true strength. God doesn't always feel as near and our prayers are not so quickly answered, so we must learn to walk by faith. No longer babied, we are thrust out into the wider world with its opportunities, difficulties and dangers that we might learn to overcome them. Your main assignment in this stage is to learn to turn from your own strength and reasoning and put on the Lord's strength. This is a long stage for most, but if we master it, God has another stage for us.

The final stage is the spiritual father or mother stage. This is the goal of our spiritual journey. At this stage *"we know Him who has been from the beginning"* (vs. 13). For years this verse confused me because I thought it was referring to God the Father. Didn't the little children and young men know God already? Years later, I saw that the key to understanding this was in the first chapter of this same epistle, *"What was from the beginning, what we have heard, what we have seen with our eyes, what we have look at and touched with our hand, concerning the Word of Life"* (I John 1:1, John 1:1-3). The disciples had not seen the Father with their eyes or touched Him with their hands, but they had seen and touched Jesus. They had walked with Jesus, sat at His feet as He taught, worked with Him and been His instruments in doing great works. They had faced danger with him, been rejected with Him and stood with Him in His trials (Luke 22:28). Therefore, He no longer considered them as mere servants but as friends (John 15:15). Just like them, we come to know Jesus progressively as we take up our cross daily, walk with Him, meditate on His Word, obey Him, serve Him and endure persecution and rejection for Him. You can't fully understand Jesus until you become like Him. We believe in Jesus when we first receive Him, but only through faithfulness over time do we come to know Him (John 6:68-69). Your main assignment is to lay your life down for those *spiritually younger* that they might come to maturity. Fathers and mothers, stay faithful in these difficult days when so many (even in the church) don't want to hear God's truth. You are needed and your faithfulness will be the foundation for a better future.

When you understand the spiritual stage you are in, then you can better understand the things you are going through and know how to respond. In the church, there are spiritual little children, young men/women and mothers and fathers. Treat each one according to the spiritual stage they are in. Be patient and gentle with the little children, encourage the young men/women as they battle and learn to overcome in the Lord's strength, and listen humbly and value the wisdom and advice of the mothers and fathers.

Prayer- Help me understand the stage I am in so I may better fulfill my assignment. Help me treat the little children, the young men/women and the fathers and mothers in the appropriate way.

Day 41

The Blame Game

"As He passed by, He saw a man blind from birth. And His disciples asked Him, "Rabbi, who sinned, this man or his parents, that he would be born blind?" Jesus answered, "It was neither that this man sinned, nor his parents; but it was so that the works of God might be displayed in him. We must work the works of Him who sent Me as long as it is day; night is coming when no one can work. While I am in the world, I am the Light of the world." When He had said this, He spat on the ground, and made clay of the spittle, and applied the clay to his eyes, and said to him, "Go, wash in the pool of Siloam" (which is translated, Sent). So he went away and washed, and came back seeing." John 9:1-7

The disciples ask Jesus the blame question. The Rabbis all agreed that suffering was a result of sin, so in the case of a seemingly innocent baby born blind, who was to blame? Various rabbis put forward differing arguments about who to blame. Today, billions of dollars are spent in courtrooms and congressional hearings to determine who to blame? There are countless heated arguments and pointed fingers in homes across America and across our television and computer screens in the quest to find who is to blame. The problem with blaming goes back to the Garden of Eden when Adam first blamed Eve and then Eve blamed the Serpent for their eating from the forbidden tree (Gen. 3:10-13).

Why did the disciples want to know who to blame? It was because they felt powerless to help the man. It is only when people don't know how to solve a problem that assigning blame becomes important. Note how different Jesus' approach is. He brushes aside the question of blame and said that both explanations were wrong. Jesus knew that every problem is an opportunity for God's power and goodness to be displayed. Knowing this He set about fixing the problem rather than fixing the blame. Before we can get trapped in the fruitless blame game, we must first doubt God's promises and loving concern for us. If we truly trust God with our problems, why do we get caught up in affixing blame? The problem with blaming others is that it tends to cripple us more than help us, because it can make us feel like powerless victims. Playing the blame game can make us miss out on God's wonderful works. Rather than sit passively by and talk about who to blame, Jesus went to work. Many times we sit discouraged and frozen before problems because we continually think of ourselves as helpless victims. But our real problem is a faith problem. We lack the faith and courage to act as Jesus did.

Note how Jesus solved this man's problem. He used something very ordinary to do a miracle. What is more ordinary than mud? If we are to see God's works, we must first believe that God can use the very ordinary to do the extraordinary. Everything He needed was right at His feet. God can start your deliverance or breakthrough in the very circumstances you find yourself. We must be willing to start right where we are with what we have. It may not seem like we have much but we always have enough to get started. Everything Foothills Church is today began as two small Bible studies in two homes. If God is working with you, even mud can bring forth a miracle.

The next curious thing Jesus did was to put the mud in the blind man's eye and tell Him to wash it out in a pool some distance away. Now the man probably wondered, *"Why did He just put mud in my eye? He just made things worse. I am still blind but now my eye feels uncomfortable and I look foolish."* He may have wondered *"Why do I have to walk blindly to that distant pool? Why can't I wash out my eye with the water jug next to me?"* The reason was because the miracle wouldn't come from the mud but from the man's obedience. He could have become offended by Jesus' method. He could have stopped short of going to the pool and washed His eyes in some nearer water source. But if he had done so, He would not have been healed. He had to follow Jesus' instruction even if He didn't understand it, even if his natural mind resisted. Many don't get their deliverance because they draw back from full obedience. It is always easier to fall back into feeling like a victim and playing the blame game than to move forward by forgiving others, trusting God or doing what might seem difficult and risky.

A woman said to me, "I hate the person that my husband has made me become." Unfortunately, as long as she believes that she is barred from growing as a person. If she is not responsible for her actions, then she has no power to change. She will always remain a victim with her life, controlled by someone else. Never say, "So and so ruined my life" because no one on earth has that power. The truth is that your life is in the hands of an all-powerful Being who loves you and tells you to call Him Father. He can redeem any situation and empower you to overcome any mistreatment or hardship. But He can only do this if you quit playing the blame game and ask Him to show you what He would have you do.

We must stop fearing problems and hardships and resenting those who we believe caused them. Biologists talk about "The Adversity Principle." They have long recognized that no species flourishes under habitual ease and well-being. Plants and animals need some stress in order to become strong and healthy. For instance, trees planted in wet regions never develop strong root systems and so blow down in a windstorm. All life seems to need some struggle or adversity in order to thrive. In a recent survey 87% of respondents said that a painful event (such as death of a loved one, illness or lay off) caused them to find a more positive meaning in life. James 1:2-4 tells us to rejoice in our trials because they strengthen our faith, produce endurance and bring us to maturity. Wasting time and energy blaming others is a dead end but trusting in God's grace is the road to life, peace and growth. Now think of some situation where you are blaming someone else for your problems. Ask God how He wants you to view the problem and how you can trust in Him to overcome it. What Bible promises can help direct you and sustain overcoming faith in you? How can you approach the situation differently and glorify God?

Prayer- I confess that I have blamed others for my problems rather than looked to You for help and deliverance. I want to forgive those I have been embittered toward and ask You to touch them in Your love. Thank You for being my faithful Helper and Friend. Help me to accept hardships and mistreatment as doorways to growth and maturity in You.

Be Ready

"Then the kingdom of heaven will be comparable to ten virgins, who took their lamps and went out to meet the bridegroom. Five of them were foolish, and five were prudent. For when the foolish took their lamps, they took no oil with them, but the prudent took oil in flasks along with their lamps. Now while the bridegroom was delaying, they all got drowsy and began to sleep. But at midnight there was a shout, 'Behold, the bridegroom! Come out to meet him.' Then all those virgins rose and trimmed their lamps. The foolish said to the prudent, 'Give us some of your oil, for our lamps are going out.' But the prudent answered, 'No, there will not be enough for us and you too; go instead to the dealers and buy some for yourselves.' And while they were going away to make the purchase, the bridegroom came, and those who were ready went in with him to the wedding feast; and the door was shut. Later the other virgins also came, saying, 'Lord, lord, open up for us.' But he answered, 'Truly I say to you, I do not know you.' Be on the alert then, for you do not know the day nor the hour."
Matthew 25:1-13

This is a parable about being ready. Ten bridesmaids have gathered to welcome the groom. The tradition was for the groom to set out hours before the wedding and walk through the village where people would greet him and invite him into their homes to celebrate the upcoming wedding. Depending on the amount of hospitality, this could take a long time. Next, he would visit the bride's home. This is where the bridesmaids were waiting to escort him into the home with their lamps lit. The groom took longer than the bridesmaids anticipated and they fell asleep. Five of the ten missed the wedding. What was the difference between the two groups?

First, notice it wasn't in their intentions. They all had good intentions to welcome the groom. Good intentions are universal. Every student graduating intends to be a success, every couple getting married intends to have a lifelong relationship of love and happiness, every parent looking into the eyes of their newborn intends to be a good parent and every person coming up out of the baptismal waters intends to be a faithful follower of Christ. Having good intentions is not the issue. It's not what determines how life turns out. This parable points out the two most important determiners in success and failure. The first is character. Five of the bridesmaids were wise and five were foolish. The second key is preparation. The two groups differed in their preparation. After more than 40 years in ministry, I have seen that these two things, character and preparation, are what separates people.

As to their character, we read that 5 were wise. Wisdom is what prepares you to succeed in life. Many chase after knowledge. Our colleges and universities are full of people pursuing knowledge. But wisdom is greater. It is more decisive. Wisdom is the understanding and skill to live life successfully. It's been said that knowledge is knowing that a tomato is a fruit and wisdom is knowing not to put it in a fruit salad. Wisdom comes from not leaning on your own understanding but leaning upon a greater understanding (Prov. 3:5-6). It comes from a commitment to turn to the Bible to find answers and perspectives. It allows you to live in such a way that you are surrounded by God's blessing and favor. It allows you to live in harmony with God great universal laws so that they work for you and not against you. On the other hand, foolishness is ignoring God's counsel. It is leaning upon your own understanding and insisting upon your own way. It is listening to the philosophies and opinions of fallible humans over God's Word. Therefore, it means that God's great Laws will often work against you.

The specific reason the 5 were called wise was because they were prepared in case things didn't go as they planned. They brought extra oil in case the bridegroom was late. Part of wisdom is acknowledging the fact that life often doesn't go according to plan. There are often delays, setbacks, unforeseen factors and unexpected events. Few things in my life worked out just as I planned - and often that was a good thing. People sometimes think they are prepared when actually *they are only prepared if everything goes exactly to plan.* The 5 foolish bridesmaids thought they were prepared, but only if the groom came according to their schedule. They weren't prepared for a delay and they ran out of oil. *The truth is that life is more determined by the unexpected than by what you expect.* It's how you respond to these unexpected situations that largely determines how your life will turn out. Making plans is essential, but developing trust in God for when things don't go according to plan is even more important because you will spend much of your life dealing with the unplanned. When things didn't go the way I planned, I would be disappointed but then I would trust God and it would eventually work out, often better than I ever hoped. Few things will come as easily or quickly as you hope. Part of preparation is developing the ability to persevere through delays and setbacks.

The famous American sprinter, Michael Johnson, holder of 4 Olympic gold medals and 8 world championships said, "Life is often compared to a marathon, but I think it is more like being a sprinter- long stretches of hard work and preparation punctuated by brief moments in which we are given the opportunity to perform." You hear people talk of "defining moments in life," but it's not true that such defining moments make us who we are. Rather, defining moments merely reveal our preparation. If we are prepared, then we succeed in those moments; if not, we fail.

The future is unknown. The 10 bridesmaids faced an unknown and uncertain night. They all had lamps lit and were full of joy and expectation. But only 5 were prepared to enter. What are you doing to prepare yourself? Do you have a plan for personal growth and spiritual preparation? It must start with a devotional life of prayer and Bible study. It must include increasing your life skills by reading books, listening to podcasts and spending time with people who inspire and stretch you. Your character and preparation will largely determine what God entrusts to you.

Prayer - Help me to go beyond mere good intentions. Help me to humbly prepare myself with wisdom and good character so I will be ready for every test and opportunity. Help me to develop a deep trust in You so I am not shaken when the unexpected happens.

Day 43

Two Sons

"A man had two sons, and he came to the first and said, 'Son, go to work today in the vineyard.' And he answered, 'I will not'; but afterwards he regretted it and went. The man came to the second and said the same thing, and he answered, 'I will, sir'; but he did not go. Which of the two did the will of the Father?"
Matthew 21:28-31

In reading the above passage, two obvious questions come to mind. First, why did the one son say "yes" to his father if he wasn't going to follow through and do it? Second, why did the other son change his mind after first saying "no?" The son who first said "yes" was just conforming to everyone's expectation. He said what he was supposed to say, what his father and others wanted to hear. He lived for the approval of others and so conformed outwardly. But in the end, he didn't follow through because his answer didn't really come from his heart. Why did the other son first say "no?" We can't know for sure; perhaps he had made other plans, or had just had a fight with his father, or was just having a bad day. Later, after having time to cool off and reflect, he did what he knew was right. You see, he lived from the inside out and was guided by his values and his identity as his father's son. In the end, only he was able to obey and please his father. He lived like a son but his brother acted like a slave.

These two sons represent two different types of believers. Either we are living out of a transformed heart or we are driven by pressures and expectations from the outside. Romans 12:2 points out the difference, *"And do not be conformed to this world, but be transformed by the renewing of your mind."* To conform means to be pressed into shape by outward pressures and the need for approval. Conformity is always based upon fear: fear of rejection, fear of failure, fear of not having enough or of being left out. But transformation comes through love. I John 4:18 says, *"Perfect love casts out fear... the one who fears is not perfected in love."* To live in fear of circumstances or the need for acceptance is to be live like a slave. Only one thing can stop you from feeling and living like a slave and that is when you are transformed by God's love and are thus able to live as a son or daughter. The sad fact is that many Christians still live as slaves. Until you learn to live secure in God's love, you will always be laboring for acceptance and security. Slaves work and serve out of fear - fear of being punished or of being rejected or of not having enough. Ever since Adam and Eve rebelled against God, all people have been born with a slave's mentality. It is what comes natural to us. It's why people do what they do. It's why people lie, steal, fight and abuse drugs and alcohol.

God sent us Jesus so we would no longer live as slaves, *"so that He might redeem those who were under the Law, that we might receive the adoption as sons. Because you are sons, God sent forth the Spirit of His Son into our hearts crying, 'Abba Father! Therefore, you are no longer a slave but a son; and if a son, then an heir through God"* (Gal. 4:4-7). What a wonderful truth, I am not longer a slave but a son/daughter and an heir. I belong, I am loved and have a wonderful inheritance from God. Love has replaced fear in my heart. Getting adopted changes your life forever. In Kenya, where we have a large ministry, the streets are full of orphans. They live on the streets where they beg and steal. They have no home, no last name and no inheritance, so they pass their time sniffing glue. But if they get adopted, everything changes. God says, "I adopted you; live like my sons and daughters" (Eph. 5:1). God's children do right, not out of fear, but out of a sense of being loved and belonging.

You can tell when a Christian is still living as a slave. When a slave is called to serve or give, inwardly they resent it and try to get by with doing the minimum. But when a son or daughter serves, they do so out of love and joy because they know they are investing in what belongs to them because they are an heir (Luke 6:38). As heirs, the riches of the Kingdom belong to us!

There are two basic motivators in life: fear and love. Either you are motivated by fear because of all the things you cannot control, or you are motivated out of an experience of God's love as His adopted child. Being adopted by God sets us free from fear and slavery, "For you have not received a spirit of slavery leading to fear again, but you have received a spirit of adoption as sons by which we cry out, 'Abba! Father'" (Rom. 8:15). Repeat this: "I will not be afraid in my Father's world. I will not live like a slave but as a son/daughter. I will live by following Jesus' words because then I will be His disciple and I will live free" (John 8:31-33).

Some Christians don't believe they are fully adopted children of God. They believe they have lived too wickedly, done so many bad things or are so broken that they are unfit. They forget that adoption is a completely undeserved gift. There is no one so good that they deserve it, and there is no one so bad that they are disqualified. Slavery is not what we were created for and so everyone wants to escape it. Jesus came and lived as a Son so everyone came to Him because they, too, wanted to live like a son and not a slave. When you truly live like a son or daughter, you make the whole world thirsty for what you have because all people want to escape being a slave.

Prayer - Thank You for making me Your son/daughter, as a gift of Your love, despite my unworthiness. Thank You, Jesus, for making it possible by being my Savior. Help me to live every day as a son/daughter without fear or compromise.

The Cry Heard In Heaven

"Now it came about in the course of those many days that the King of Egypt died. And the sons of Israel sighed because of the bondage, and they cried out; and their cry for help because of their bondage rose up to God. So God heard their groaning; and God remembered His covenant with Abraham, Isaac, and Jacob." Exodus 2:23-24

Thus begins the deliverance of Israel from bondage in Egypt. The Israelites sighed, groaned and cried out in their bondage and oppression and God heard their groaning in heaven, took notice and brought about their deliverance. He sent Moses to them and brought 10 great plagues upon the Egyptians until Pharaoh let them go. But it all started with their groaning. Likewise, a number of times during the 400 years covered in the Book of Judges, God delivered his people because of their *"groaning"* (Judges 2:18). In the Bible *"groaning"* and *"sighing"* are inward reactions to suffering, injustice and ungodliness. It is an expression of mental, emotional and spiritual duress and grief because things are not right.

As Christians today, all of us feel this inward duress at the current state of our society. The Bible tells us, *"When the righteous increase, the people rejoice, but when a wicked man rules, people groan"* (Prov. 29:2). When unrighteousness and falsehood are entrenched in the ruling places of society, people will suffer and groan. This is especially true of those who have the Spirit of God. Everything that is of God groans under ungodliness, until godliness is established. If a person doesn't have a deep grief and sorrow over the state of our society, then they do not have the Spirit of God. We read that Lot, Abraham's brother, *"felt his righteous soul tormented day after day"* by the lawless deeds of Sodom where he lived (II Peter 2:7-8). We read of the Apostle Paul in Athens that, *"his spirit was being provoked within him as he was observing the city full of idols"* (Acts 17:16). The awakened spirit within us sighs and groans under the weight of ungodliness. We simply can't accept or make peace with ungodliness. It's proof we belong to God.

In 582BC, God judged Jerusalem for her wickedness. Nebuchadnezzar, the King of Babylon, destroyed the city and carried off the survivors. Just before that event, God gave Ezekiel the prophet a vision of the Lord giving a commission to an angel, *"Go through the midst of the city, even through the midst of Jerusalem, and put a mark on the foreheads of the men who sigh and groan over all the abominations which are being committed in its midst"* (Ezekiel 9:4). These people received a spiritual mark of protection because they had not accommodated themselves to the wickedness but had remained loyal to the Lord's ways. We see the same thing in the Book of Revelation (Rev. 7:3; 9:4; 14:1). Being the light of the world and the salt of the earth during a time of growing darkness and corruption can seem like a heavy burden. But our godly reaction to that corruption is part of the Lord's redemptive purpose.

The important thing is what we do with this inward groaning and sorrow. In the instance cited above, Paul went that very day and began preaching in the market at Athens and he got a harvest (Acts 17:17, 34). The Israelites turned their groaning into crying out to God and were delivered. Lot did nothing and as a result ended up suffering great loss. This inward groaning or pressure can't be ignored. Sooner or later, we must give voice to it seeking relief. Either we will complain, blame and find fault, which is giving voice to the Accuser (Satan), or we will turn that groaning towards Heaven and intercede for our society, which is giving voice to the Great Intercessor, Jesus (Heb. 7:25; Rom. 8:34; Luke 13: 6-9). God wants our inward groaning to become redemptive. The Holy Spirit Himself helps us turn this groaning into effective prayer. The Holy Spirit joins His groaning to ours and it rises up to God and He hears us (Rom. 8:23, 26).

If you carry Jesus' Spirit, you can't enjoy the entertainment of today. You don't laugh at the popular comedians and are grieved if you watch the latest sensation streaming into America's homes. You are distressed by much of the news of the day. Many don't understand you and consider you out of step. They mock your sorrow and concern and consider some of your ideas to be hateful and dangerous. Inwardly your spirit groans throughout the day. Jesus felt this same inward duress and heaviness because of the unbelief and wickedness around Him (Matt. 17:17; Mark 8:12; Luke 19:41). Sharing in this struggle is part of our fellowship with Jesus. It gives us an opportunity to serve Him. We groan under the ungodliness, but if we turn that groaning into intercession and service Jesus can use it to bring deliverance and revival.

Prayer - In carrying this inward groaning against ungodliness, I am entering into the "fellowship of Your suffering" Paul spoke about. Give me the grace to endure it in the same manner You did. Help me to become a redemptive part of Your plan by turning it into prayer and service. Help me to love the lost as You do and to have faith through difficult times as You did. Help me to find my relief and joy in You at all times.

Day 45

Before and After

"And although you were formerly alienated and hostile in mind, engaged in evil deeds, yet He has not reconciled you in His fleshly body through death, in order to present you before Him holy and blameless and beyond reproach." Colossians 1:21-22

People sometimes wonder, "Why is it so hard to live a Christian life?" Why does doing wrong come so easy and doing right seem so hard? Why is it so easy to lose your temper, give in to temptation and hold grudges and so hard to forgive, admit we are wrong and prefer others?" Well, the wonderful truth is that God's Spirit can change us so that doing the right thing becomes natural and joyful. The question is, how does that happen?

All of us have seen "before" and "after" pictures in ads in magazines and television. They show, for instance, the wonderful changes that a diet product can produce. Did you know that the above passage is a "before" and "after" picture of a believer? It shows how we can change. Verse 21 shows us the "before" picture, and verse 22 the "after" picture - what we want to become. Let's look at the "after" picture in verse 22 first. Please note three characteristics:

We are *"holy."* Holy means "set apart." God has set us apart and appointed us to express His goodness and love. Holiness is reflecting the qualities of Jesus and walking in His ways.

The second attribute is *"blameless."* Jesus' blood and righteousness makes us fully acceptable to God. His Spirit then works to transform us so we live righteously and blamelessly before others.

The third attribute is *"beyond reproach."* God causes us to live above reproach, so that we are respected. Our reputation opens doors for us and silences gossip. These three attributes make up the "after" picture. This is how God sees us on the day we are born again. From that day on God's Spirit works in us until we are transformed into His image. To understand how this transformation can happen, we must understand the "before" picture.

In verse 21 we find the natural condition of the unsaved or unregenerate person. It's where we all begin. Notice the attributes: *alienated, hostile in mind and engaged in evil deeds.*

In our natural state our mind is *hostile* to God and full of wrong ideas. When I was lost, I thought God's demands were too hard. I thought I could not live a Christian life. It was a lie but it kept me from God. My education made me doubt God's existence. Early experiences of rejection and disappointment caused me to develop a negative view of life, full of fear, self -protection and unbelief. God's solution is to gain a "renewed mind" (Rom. 12:2), through Bible reading and the work of the Holy Spirit. A renewed mind allows you to believe and trust God.

Next, we were *"alienated* from God" in our affections. God's ways seemed alien, foreign and unappealing. We drew back from humility, purity and preferring others. Like many aliens in our country today, who were born and raised in a foreign culture, we were more comfortable with the worldly culture we were raised in than with the culture of God's Kingdom. But as we obediently and diligently followed God's ways and saw the benefits, we become assimilated to the new culture and begin to love God's ways.

Finally, we were engaged in evil deeds and sinful habits that kept us from God, living in defeat and bondage. If I want to walk in fellowship with Jesus and see my life transformed, I must change my habits and lifestyle. With the Holy Spirit's help, I displace ungodly old habits and practices with new godly ones. Instead of being drunk with alcohol, I learn to be filled with the Holy Spirit through thankfulness and worship (Eph. 5:18-19). Instead of going to clubs at night, I participate in church events and Christian fellowship. Instead of reading romance novels I read the Bible and Christian literature. In other words, instead of activities that grieve the Holy Spirit, I replace them with activities in which the Holy Spirit can work to transform me. As I do so my appetites and desires change.

One man sits in a bar and thinks, "I have absolutely no desire to go to church." Another man sits in church and thinks, "I have absolutely no desire to go to a bar." I have been both of those men. God changed me from the first man to the second through His Word and the work of the Spirit. II Corinthians 5:17 says, *"Therefore if anyone is in Christ, he is a new creature; the old things have passed away; new things have come."* A caterpillar crawls in the dirt. A beautiful butterfly flies thru the air. Every butterfly was once a caterpillar. Every caterpillar can become a butterfly. The caterpillar is what we were- *alienated, hostile in mind and engaged in evil deeds.* But the butterfly is *holy, blameless and beyond reproach.*

All Christians are living somewhere between the "before" and "after" pictures. Sanctification is the process of spiritual transformation until we become increasingly like Jesus. It's the journey from what I was, to what God has declared me to be. Let God complete His wonderful work of transformation in you.

Prayer - I desire to live a life that is holy, blameless and beyond reproach. Help me to live a life focused on Your Word and yielded to the Holy Spirit. I want to be transformed into the image of Jesus.

Finding God's Will

"Trust in the Lord with all your heart; do not depend upon your own understanding. Seek His will in all that you do, and He will show you which path to take." Proverbs 3:5-6 (NLT)

Do you believe God has a plan for your life? Do you believe He has a preferred path that includes such things as your career, whether to marry, who to marry, where to live, what church to attend, what ministry to be involved in and even where to retire? Have you ever prayed for God to reveal His will for you? Most Christians have.

Now imagine you held an envelope in your hand that revealed God's specific plan for the rest of your life. Would you want to open it and know its contents? There is just one catch. Once you open it, you are responsible to obey what is inside. The plans in that envelope would have to supersede any plans or desires you presently have. Would you still open it? Consider that question carefully.

One reason we struggle to discover God's will for our life is that we are double-minded about it. We want to know it for some reasons; for instance, we believe that God's will would be best for us in the long run – that it would result in the most fruitful and blessed life. But, on the other hand, we draw back from it because we fear His plans might differ from what we presently desire, and might involve challenges and difficulties we don't want to face.

Therefore, we are double-minded. James 1:7 tells us that when we are double-minded, we shouldn't expect to receive God's wisdom.

Many turn from truly seeking God's will because they foolishly think that their own plans will make them happier. This reveals a lack of faith in God and His love for us. Romans 12:2 tells us that God's will is *"good, pleasing and perfect."* His plan for you is the best plan, one that will bless and satisfy you and is perfect in the light of eternity.

An important principle to remember is that God reveals His will to us progressively. He only reveals to us what we need to know at the time. Proverbs 4:18 says, *"But the path of the righteous is like the light of dawn, that shines brighter and brighter until the full day."* As you start down God's path for you, the first rays of early morning light allow you to see only a little way ahead. But as you continue down that path in obedience, more light comes to you.

In other words, it is only by walking in the part of God's will that you know, that you will come to learn the part of God's will that is yet unknown to you. As you obey what you know, He will reveal more of His will for you as you need it. The first part of God's will we must walk in is His general will for all Christians that is revealed in the Bible. This includes such things as living in purity, humility, forgiveness and love. If we will not walk in these things, we will not be in a place to receive specific and personal revelation for our life. Ask yourself, "How am I doing in following God's commands in Scripture?"

Unlike what some people think, being in God's will doesn't mean a life of problem-free sailing. God's leading will sometimes take us through difficulties and even mistreatment by others. Remember that the ultimate purpose of God leading us is not for our short-term ease and comfort but that we become conformed to the image of His Son, Jesus. Difficulties don't mean you missed God or are out of His will. They are part of learning to *"walk by faith and not by sight"* (II Cor. 5:7). As we do, our faith grows, as we see God's faithfulness to us, and we become more Christ-like. The real test of whether we are in God's will is not our present circumstances, but rather, do we have God's peace (Phil. 4:9)?

God is calling each of us to the adventure of walking in His will. Discovering God's will for us is part of our inheritance as children of God (Rom. 8:14; Ps. 32:8). But remember that we must first be committed to do God's will, even before we know what it is, and we must be faithful to obey what God has already shown us.

Prayer – I want to know Your will so I may walk in it and please You. I believe that Your will is the best and most satisfying for me. Help me to have the humility, love and courage to seek out and follow Your will in every circumstance.

Why Does God Test Us?

"You shall remember all the way which the Lord your God has led you in the wilderness these forty years, that He might humble you, testing you, to know what was in your heart, whether you would keep His commandments or not. He humbled you and let you be hungry, and fed you with manna which you did not know, nor did your fathers know, that He might make you understand that man does not live by bread alone, but man lives by everything that proceeds out of the mouth of the Lord. In the wilderness He fed you manna which your fathers did not know, that He might humble you and that He might test you, to do good for you in the end."
Deuteronomy 8:2,3,16

Almost nobody likes tests. Tests can be very difficult and challenging; they can make us worry and stress out. Yet, the fact is, we must all face and pass tests to advance a grade in school, get a job or promotion, or obtain various licenses. Even God tests us. The truth is, in both the natural and the spiritual there is no advancement without passing tests. This can help us answer the question we sometimes ask, "Why is God letting this happen to me?"

Likely, almost all of us are facing some test because God wants to bless and promote us, and that requires passing tests. We need to recognize God's tests, rather than resent them, because there's great reward in passing them. They are a doorway to advancement and blessing.

Reread verse 2 above. It says that God led them, testing them to know what was in their hearts. We learn that in leading us, God will take us through tests. Encountering a hardship, setback or suffering doesn't mean you must have missed God or done something wrong. Encountering tests are an important part of His leading us. The Israelites were clearly led out of Egypt into the wilderness with the parting of the Red Sea and the pillar of fire going before them. Yet on their journey they faced many tests, such as no water, no food, and being attacked. It says that He tested them *"to know what was in your heart."* The Israelites would come to know what was in their hearts by their failure to obey God's Commandments in the test. They learned the truth about themselves and their need for God.

Many of us have a conflict of interest with God about the point of our life. We want God to give us a life of ease, prosperity and happiness. But, God, above all, wants to shape us into the image of His Son. He wants us to truly become sons and daughters. We want blessings in this life. God wants that for us, too, but even more He wants to prepare us for even greater rewards in the next. God always sees our lives from an eternal perspective. God said the tests were to teach us *"that man does not live by bread alone, but by everything that proceeds out of the mouth of the Lord"* (vs. 3). In facing tests, we learn the inadequacy of earthly things, the greatness of God's riches, and especially our need to follow His Word.

In verse 16 we read that God's tests are *"so that He might humble you."* Pride means to be focused on yourself and to place your faith in yourself. Humility means to be focused on and place your faith in something greater than yourself. God wants us to learn that we are not enough. God wants us to learn to live out of His love, strength and wisdom. Only then can we become His overcoming sons and daughters.

In verse 16 we learn a very critical lesson. It says that God gave them the manna to humble and test them. Now, no doubt, they received the manna as a great blessing. They were hungry and God gave them miraculous bread to eat. No doubt they woke up that morning, saw the manna, and said, "Hallelujah!" What they didn't realize was that they were being tested. What we must realize is that every blessing is also a test. Not all tests are unpleasant or unwelcome. Some come in the form of great blessings. The test may come as a windfall of money, a promotion at work, public recognition, or someone of the opposite sex showing interest in us. The test is how you handle the blessing. A person who gains a big inheritance is being tested as surely as a person who is facing a financial hardship. The hearts of both will be exposed in how they deal with the test. The future blessedness of each will depend on whether they pass their respective tests.

Passing tests brings blessings and advancement. In verse 16 we read that the purpose of tests is that God *"might do you good in the end."* Even though most tests are unwelcome, they are necessary. Because there are great dangers and responsibilities that come with promotion and blessings, we must first be tested and approved, lest the blessing become our undoing. Tests are the doorway to blessing and promotion. Therefore, we should not fear tests, or run from them. Instead, we should, *"Consider it all joy, my brethren, when you encounter various trials"* (James 1:2). Are you being severely tested? Remember, great testing brings great blessing and advancement.

Prayer – Thank You for tests that come into my life that help conform me into Christ's image and prepare me for future advancement and blessing. Help me to not fear or resent them, but to receive them with joy and to have the faith and humility to grow though them.

Day 48

Overcoming Hatred

"Never pay back evil for evil to anyone. Respect what is right in the sight of all men. If possible, so far as it depends on you, be at peace with all men. Never take your own revenge, beloved, but leave room for the wrath of God, for it is written, "VENGEANCE IS MINE, I WILL REPAY," says the Lord. "BUT IF YOUR ENEMY IS HUNGRY, FEED HIM, AND IF HE IS THIRSTY, GIVE HIM A DRINK; FOR IN SO DOING YOU WILL HEAP BURNING COALS ON HIS HEAD." Do not be overcome by evil, but overcome evil with good."
Romans 12:17-21

We read above that, to the extent possible, we are to *"be at peace with all men."* This is our calling. We are called to bring God's peace. Jesus said there is a great blessing in being a peacemaker. He said that peacemakers *"shall be called sons of God"* (Matt. 5:9). In bringing peace we show forth God's nature, for He is a peacemaker. Jesus is called the "Prince of Peace" (Is. 9:6). Jesus brings peace to the human heart, peace between people, and most importantly, peace with God.

Now, if we are to be peacemakers, we must be proactive. We must sow seeds of peace all around us. James 3:18 (CEV) tells us *"When peacemakers plant seeds of peace, they will harvest justices."* Seeds of peace are acts of kindness, encouraging words, extending forgiveness, practical helps and the like. When we plant such seeds, we reap right relationships, justice and tranquility.

Our world is in great need of peace. We can plant such seeds among our neighbors and coworkers and even those who view us as enemies. These seeds are powerful through God who works through peacemakers.

We read in the passage above that we are to live in peace with all men *"so far as it depends upon you."* Sometimes people refuse to live in peace with us. But even when people refuse the seeds of peace we offer. and harden their hearts, God can still work if we let Him. We must not respond to the angry words and actions of others with angry words of our own. We are to *"never take your own revenge."* Jesus taught us to *"bless those who persecute you"* (Rom. 12:16). We are to act with kindness, giving food and drink to our opponents when they need it. When we do this, it says that we will *"heap burning coals"* on their head. What does this mean?

When someone treats you wrong and you return kindness, God opens up the windows of Heaven and reigns conviction upon them. God reveals to the person the ugliness of their own heart when they see the love and goodness in your heart. Our part is to show love, kindness and forgiveness, and God's part is to pour out conviction upon them. Nothing is more natural than to strike back at those who hurt us. But if we do this, we will only escalate the hatred and strife. But if we do it God's way. we can *"overcome evil with good."* First, you must settle it in your heart. once for all. that you give up your right to "get even," and then you must look for opportunities to repay evil with kindness. If you will do these two things, you will have the thrill of seeing what God can do. You will find that this principle is one of our spiritual weapons (II Cor. 10:3-5).

Now think of your own circumstances. Where can you plant seeds of peace? Even in the most unpromising-looking fields you can get a harvest. God's principle is powerful. God calls you to be a peacemaker.

Prayer – I want to be Your peacemaker. Help open my eyes to see the opportunities to sow Your seeds of peace. Thank You for giving me the love and patience to return kindness and love to those who mistreat me and so overcome evil with good.

Two Trees

*"Trust in the L*ORD *with all your heart and do not lean on your own understanding." Proverbs 3:5*

Each of us faces a question every day – in fact, we face it a number of times each day. That question is, "Will I put my trust in my feelings and understanding, or will I put my trust in God despite my feelings, perceptions and understanding?" Only one of these paths is the path to blessings. The decision boils down to, "Will I allow my limited and untrustworthy feelings and reasoning to rob me, or will I allow God's unlimited and perfect wisdom and love to lead me into blessings and life?"

This is the choice that was before Adam and Eve when they faced the two trees in the Garden. The Tree of Life represented living in union with and dependence upon God, who is the source of life. It involved being enlightened and led by the Spirit of God. The Tree of the Knowledge of Good and Evil, on the other hand, represented deciding good and evil for themselves, depending upon their reasoning, feelings, and judgment. This always brings separation and alienation from God. As we know, they chose wrong, and it brought brokenness, division and suffering. Every day we face this same temptation to replace God's truth and understanding with our own understanding.

God had said not to eat from the Tree of the Knowledge of Good and Evil, but, instead, Eve looked upon the tree and decided that *"it was good for food… a delight to the eyes and… desirable"* (Gen. 3:6), therefore she ate of it. In doing so, she came to know defeat and loss.

But Jesus was different. He showed us the way to victory. It was prophesied of Jesus that, *"He will delight in the fear of the Lord, and He will not judge by what His eyes see, nor make a decision by what His ears hear"* (Is. 11:3). Instead, He feared God, delighted in Him, and was led by the same Spirit that has been given to you and me. Adam and Eve ate from the Tree of the Knowledge of Good and Evil, but Jesus continually ate from the Tree of Life. And so should we.

Which tree are you eating from? If you have to understand everything before you can obey, you are eating from the Tree of Knowledge. But if you can go beyond your doubts and worship and obey God, you are eating from the Tree of Life, and you will know God as your unfailing source.

We become overcomers by choosing God's truth over our emotions and reasoning. Going against your own reasoning is not being irrational; it allows you to be super-rational. It allows you to go beyond the limits of your own understanding and draw from God's understanding.

The Christian life is a continual turning to God and His riches, which means a turning away from self-centeredness (pride), self-protection (fear) and self-sufficiency (rebellion and unbelief). It is done step-by-step and moment-by-moment, which is why our Christian life is referred as a "walk by faith" (II Cor. 5:7; Gal. 5:16). In this way we can live in His love and power every day.

Prayer – I desire to eat every day from the Tree of Life. I want to live beyond my doubts and emotions by believing Your promises and trusting in Your faithfulness. I do not trust in my own perception or wisdom. I want to turn from my self-centeredness and live in Your love and power each day.

Bloom Wherever You Are Planted

"Thus says the Lord of hosts, the God of Israel, to all the exiles whom I have sent into exile from Jerusalem to Babylon, 'Build houses and live in them; and plant gardens and eat their produce. Take wives and become the fathers of sons and daughters, and take wives for your sons and give your daughters to husbands, that they may bear sons and daughters; and multiply there and do not decrease. Seek the welfare of the city where I have sent you into exile, and pray to the Lord on its behalf; for in it welfare you will have welfare.'"
Jeremiah 29:4-7

Have you ever been stuck far from home, or found yourself in a place or situation you wished you could escape from but couldn't? Maybe you feel that way right now? Israel was once sent into exile for 70 years. They were a defeated people living in a strange land with strange customs, subject to mistreatment and prejudice. God spoke the above words to them through the prophet Jeremiah. He told them to embrace their present, unwelcome circumstances and prosper there. They were in Babylon because King Nebuchadnezzar had invaded Israel and carried them off as prisoners, and, yet, in verse 4, God says, *"whom I have sent into exile."* God had exiled them due to their idolatry so He could bring correction to them.

Every event in our life, whether good or bad, has a visible and immediate cause. But every event also has a deeper divine purpose and the unseen hand of a Being who loves you. Now, you can choose to resent and curse the person or event that was the immediate cause of your unhappy situation. If you do, you will experience anger, discouragement and even despair. Or you can trust that God is working to bring about His purpose in your life. Romans 8:28 tells us that *"... God causes all things to work together for good to those who love God..."*

Israel's wellbeing depended on whether they would resent and despise the Babylonians for their present unhappy circumstances, or whether they would acknowledge God's loving hand and accept those very circumstances as *God's present assignment* for them to bring about His purpose. If they would accept His assignment, then He would increase, prosper and bless them in Babylon.

This is the very same decision facing many of us. Are we able to accept our circumstances as God's present assignment to bring about His purpose? The Jews were to pray for Babylon and seek its welfare. They were to seek to be a blessing to those around them. In blessing Babylon, they would also be blessed.

Wherever you find yourself is God's anointed place of blessing. Do not curse the place that God has appointed to bless you. God says, "Bless your present situation and pray for those who mistreat you." If you do, He will begin to bless you right where you find yourself: in that job, under that boss, in that city and neighborhood, etc. Daniel, Esther and Nehemiah were all blessed and prospered greatly in Babylon.

Many pray to be taken out of their circumstances; far fewer have the faith to accept those circumstances as God's present appointed place of blessing for them in this season of their life. We must accept our present assignment and pray boldly, "Right here, right now, cause me to bloom where I am planted."

No doubt the Jews struggled with guilt and regret because it was their unfaithfulness that led to their captivity. No doubt they thought, "If only we hadn't acted wickedly, if only our leaders had followed God, if only Nebuchadnezzar hadn't invaded our land." "If only" is one of the most spiritually defeating phrases in the English language. "If only I wouldn't have done this, if only this hadn't happened." In a subtle way it says God can't bless me where I am. Beautiful flowers bloom in dry deserts and high atop cold alpine mountains. You don't always get the circumstances you desire, but God can make you can bloom anywhere.

God determines the time of our assignment. After 70 years, God restored the Jews back to their homeland. God has better things ahead for us, but for now, we are to bless and be blessed right where we find ourselves.

Prayer – Forgive me for resenting my circumstances and resenting those I blame for putting me there. Help me to bless them instead. Help me to see Your purposes in my present circumstances and to trust You to bless me right where I am.

Day 51

Pop Religion

"Truly, truly, I say to you, you seek Me, not because you saw signs, but because you ate of the loaves and were filled. Do not work for the food which perishes, but for the food which endures to eternal life, which the Son of Man will give you."
John 6:26-27

Jesus spoke these words the day after feeding 5000 people with 2 fish and 5 loaves of bread. That evening Jesus slipped away and crossed over to the other side of the Sea of Galilee. In the morning the people searched and found Him. Rather than commending them for seeking Him, He gently rebuked them with the above words. He cautioned them (and us) about how easy it is to have the wrong focus and motivation in religion. They had come seeking Jesus for more food but had missed something much greater. The miraculous supply of food had been a sign. When someone takes 5 loaves and 2 fish and feeds 5000 people it means something more than just a full stomach is available; it means God has drawn near. Every blessing and gift is a sign that points beyond itself to the Giver of that gift. God is far greater and more to be desired than His gifts. God calls us to seek His Face above the gifts from His Hand.

The crowd had a popular but corrupt view of religion. I call it pop religion. Like pop music, pop art and pop psychology, it fits the current spirit, tastes and values of the day, but it's not true religion. It is concerned with seeking after the things and pleasures of this world. But Christianity is not a means to get what you want, that is a modern distortion. Christians have traditionally defined religion as the grateful and joyous fulfilling of our duties to God because of what He has first done for us. Paul warns us of falling for something that has the appearance of Christianity but not its true power. (II Tim. 3:5). He said there are many who will run to teachers and pastors who tell them what they want to hear, rather than to accept all of God's Word (II Tim. 4:3-4). What we have in much of the church today is a popular and culturally acceptable form of Christianity that is empty and lacking in power.

Pop religion affirms our desires rather than challenging them. Pop religion seeks to provide *feel good* experiences rather than a true encounter with a Holy God that produces true transformation into the image of Christ and conformity to the Bible's teaching. The power of true Christianity is not the power to gain wealth or have our desires fulfilled. Rather, it is the power to bring us before God, break sin's hold over us and change our hearts. Whenever the focus is only on God's love and affirmation and the requirement to repent is absent and when Christianity is presented as a means to self-fulfillment and success, but sacrifice for others is seldom or never mentioned, this is not true religion. When people think Jesus came to earth and died on a cross merely so they could have material prosperity and a pleasant, trouble-free life of unbroken happiness, they are not following the religion of Jesus.

Jesus required a very personal commitment, "*If anyone wishes to come after Me, he must deny himself, take us his cross daily and follow Me*" (Luke 9:23). The cost for living a true Christian life is the cross. A cross is an instrument of death. Just as Christ died on the Cross, so we must die to our sinful desires and self-centered pride, if we are to know the peace and joy of Christ's overcoming life in us. Just like the old saying, "Everybody wants to go to heaven, but nobody wants to die," just so, everybody wants to experience the new life in Christ but nobody wants to face the cross. But it is only the cross that deals with the problem of our sinful heart, which is what ultimately defeats us. The life we truly want, and the person we want to be, are waiting for us on the other side of the cross. Two things must be at work in us every day: death and resurrection life. The cross is present in anything that causes us to face our self-centered pride, lusts or fear and die to them so that the new life of Divine love, supernatural strength and the fruit of the Spirit might reign in us. To the natural mind the cross is to be avoided, but to those who embrace it, it is the doorway to the power of God (I Cor. 1:18). If there is no cross, there is no power. The cross must precede resurrection life; it was true for Jesus and it is true for us.

Many are attracted to churches that offer pop religion with its promised benefits because they are not yet ready for God's diagnosis of our problem, which is sin, and His radical solution of the cross. If we offer the world pop religion, we offer it nothing at all because the human soul will never be satisfied with anything less than Jesus. If we entice people to church with promises of financial blessings and better marriages and preach entertaining messages but do not preach in a way that will bring them face to face with the necessity of the cross, they will never be converted and thus will never know God or His power. We must avoid the influence of pop religion around us and look to the cross as our doorway to resurrection life. Rather than avoid the cross, embrace it as God's gift that brings you His victory and power.

Prayer - I desire to seek Your Face above Your gifts. I want to follow Jesus step-by-step, and decision-by-decision each day. Help me to recognize the cross at work in my life and to embrace it every day that I might know Your resurrection life within me.

Peace in a Troubled World

*"The wicked flee when no one is pursuing,
but the righteous are bold as a lion." Proverbs 28:1*

*"But the wicked are like the tossing sea, which cannot rest,
whose waves cast up mire and mud. 'There is no peace,' says my
God, 'for the wicked.'" Isaiah 57:20-21*

The above verses illustrate the difference between those who belong to God and those who have rejected Him. For the true believer, there is peace and confidence. But for those who have rejected God, there is no lasting inner peace but rather fear, anxiousness, and continuing turmoil. In 1947, two years after the end of WW II, the atomic scientists of the Manhattan project (where the first atomic bomb was produced) created a symbolic 24-hour clock, known as the "Doomsday Clock." This countdown clock represented their assessment of how near we were to worldwide nuclear annihilation. They set it at seven minutes before midnight (midnight representing nuclear extinction). Considering there are 1,440 minutes on a 24-hour clock being just seven minutes before midnight meant we were already 99.51% down the road to total destruction - a truly frightening thought. Every year they would reassess the threat and reset the clock.

As nuclear tensions decreased, environmental concerns were added into the doomsday equation. For instance, on April 22, 1970, the first Earth Day was held. At that event leading scientists told us that civilization would end in 15-30 years. Due to dropping global temperatures, we would enter a new ice age by the year 2000, and because of population growth, 200 million people would be starving to death by 1980 and that by the year 2000 there would be no crude oil left on earth. Subsequent environmental panics were the depletion of the ozone layer over the earth, the deforestation of our planet due to acid rain, plus much more. Every year, for the past 75 years, the atomic scientists have adjusted the remaining minutes on the Doomsday Clock up or down according to the threat as they perceived it. Each year, the changes were relatively small and the overall average has remained 7 minutes until midnight. For the past 75 years, they told us, every year, that we are living on the razor's edge of global catastrophe and extinction-yet here we are.

The past 75 years have been a testament to the anxiety that grips the human heart and mind when we deny God's existence and involvement in our world. Without faith we have no real security or rest - only unrelenting existential insecurity and fear. Why do secular people continually go from doomsday prediction to doomsday prediction? Think about it, God created us to thankfully receive and enjoy what He has made and then to honor and worship Him in return. Therefore, the most basic human emotion of those who have rejected their Creator is fear and guilt. Fear because they no longer believe in a loving Creator who watches over His Creation, and guilt because they have rebelled against the One who made them. Therefore, they live with a continual, subconscious expectation of calamity.

But, as believers, we should not be alarmed by their continual predictions of doom. We should remember the song that millions of children sing in Sunday school, "He's got the whole world in His hands." God wants us to rest in His goodness, faithfulness and sovereignty. Psalm 95:6-7 says, *"Come let us worship and bow down, let us kneel before the Lord our Maker, for He is our God and we are the people of His pasture and the sheep of His hand."* Those who have forgotten their Maker are like sheep without a shepherd living in constant insecurity. But we have an all-powerful Shepherd who offers us protection and rest. Jesus told us, *"Do not let your heart be troubled; believe in God, believe also in Me"* (John 14:1). Jesus gives us His peace as a gift (John 14:27). Don't let the world's agitations and fears steal from you this wonderful gift of Jesus' peace. The Devil attempts to control and drive us with fear and weaken us with despair. But God leads us with His peace and strengthens us with His joy (Isaiah 55:12; Nehemiah 8:10). Isaiah 26:3 promises us, *"The steadfast in mind You will keep in perfect peace, because he trusts in You."* We need to trust in God and learn to keep our minds steadfastly on God's love, faithfulness and sovereign control. If you do, God's peace will guard over your heart and mind (Phil. 4:7).

Prayer - Thank You for Your peace, protection and comfort in this frightened and troubled world. Forgive me for allowing the world to steal Your peace from me. Help me to live everyday as the sheep of Your hand, trusting in you completely.

Day 53

Jesus in Camouflage

"Then the righteous will answer Him, 'Lord, when did we see You hungry, and feed You, or thirsty, and give You something to drink? And when did we see You a stranger, and invite You in, or naked, and clothe You? When did we see You sick, or in prison, and come to You?' The King will answer and say to them, 'Truly I say to you to the extent that you did it to one of these brothers of Mine, even the least of them, you did it to Me.'"
Matthew 25:37-40

Our passage comes from the Great White Throne Judgment where the goats (unbelievers) are separated from the sheep after Jesus returns. The goats are rejected because they failed to recognize and accept Jesus as their Savior. The sheep (those who accepted Jesus as Savior) are rewarded because they served Jesus. What is surprising and profound is the fact that the sheep so often didn't recognize Jesus even as they served Him.

Jesus came to His people in hidden form, and they didn't recognize Him. They said, in effect, *"We don't understand; when did we feed You when You were hungry and when did You come to us as a stranger, etc.?"* One of the greatest obstacles we face as Christians is not recognizing Jesus in the people and events around us. The profound truth we must grasp is that Jesus often comes to us in hidden form.

171

The obvious question is, "Why does He do this? Why does He come to us in hidden form?" The answer is that He does it to test our hearts. If Jesus came to us in His full glory, bright as the sun, with a voice like thunder, everybody would obey Him. Unbelievers would submit to Him out of fear. Even careless Christians would serve and obey Him out of the dread of Him. But Jesus wants to test and reveal hearts, so He comes to us at unexpected and even inconvenient times, and in hidden and surprising ways.

Many in the first century world rejected Jesus because they wouldn't accept the apostles and the message they preached. Jesus told the apostles, *"He who receives you, receives Me, and he who receives Me, receives Him who sent Me"* (Matt. 10:40). It is the same today. All of us got saved because we recognized God's offer of salvation through a human that God put in our way. We recognized the voice of God through a human.

God comes to us through His human representatives. When we don't recognize Jesus when He comes to us, we miss out on a blessing. God can speak to us through a preacher's sermon, or through the counsel of a fellow believer. How often Christians fail to receive what God wants to give them because they won't accept the ministry or counsel of those He sends to them!

But, as we read in the passage above, Jesus also comes to us in a different way. Often He comes to us in the form of a person in need. He gives us the opportunity to love and serve Him through that person. We read in Hebrews 13:2, *"Do not neglect to show hospitality to strangers, for by this some have entertained angels without knowing it."* This passage has primary reference to Abraham who showed hospitality, in Genesis 18, to three strangers who turned out to be the Lord Himself with two angels. Because Abraham cared for them, God gave a wonderful promise to Abraham and allowed him to be the instrument of deliverance for his nephew, Lot. Could Jesus have already visited you this week in the form of someone needing kindness or help? Could He visit you today? Remember, it is easy to love an unseen God. It is much harder to love a fellow human in need for God's sake.

Even more amazing to consider is that Jesus can visit another person through you. You can be Jesus' hands and mouth. Jesus can even bring a sinner from darkness to light through you. There is an important lesson to be learned from this. We must be ready to serve Jesus when He comes to us in hidden form. Nurturing a right attitude and striving to always do the right thing will make sure we don't miss Jesus. We will always be prepared to serve Jesus and receive from Him when He comes to us in hidden form.

Prayer – Help me to have eyes to recognize You in all Your hidden forms. Help me to receive Your counsel and direction from the Christians and leaders You send to me. Help me to recognize the opportunities to love and serve You and those around me who are in need.

Day 54

Moses' Staff

*The Lord said to him, "What is that in your hand?" And he said,
"A staff." Then He said, "Throw it on the ground." So he threw it
on the ground, and it became a serpent; and Moses fled from
it. But the Lord said to Moses, "Stretch out your hand and grasp
it by its tail"—so he stretched out his hand and caught it, and it
became a staff in his hand. Exodus 4:2-4*

God appeared to Moses in the wilderness, in a burning bush. He
told Moses to go back to Egypt and set his people free from
slavery and lead them into the Promised Land. Moses responded
by asking, *"What if they won't listen to me or believe me?"* After
all, he was long forgotten in Egypt. He had been gone 40 years
tending sheep in the wilderness and wasn't qualified for the job.
God ignored his question and simply asked him what he had in his
hand. What he had was a shepherd's staff. His shepherd's staff
represented the knowledge and skills he had gained from 40 years
of being a shepherd. It was how he made a living for his family and
it had become his identity. When Moses held onto the staff, he
felt in control. His life seemed safe and predictable. God said to
him, *"Throw it to the ground."* In order for Moses to gain spiritual
power and credibility, he had to release his staff at the Lord's
command. He had to be willing to surrender control to God.

If we want to be God's instrument to influence others and change
our world, God first asks us, *"What is in our hand?"* That is - what

talents, knowledge, opportunities and possessions do you have? Instead of listing our inadequacies and what we lack, we must recognize the potential of what we already have because that is what the Lord will start with. Do you have a house or apartment? God says, "Great! Consider your house My embassy and yourself as My ambassador to your neighborhood. Consider the school you attend as the mission field I am sending you to. Consider yourself as a chaplain at your place of work. Oh, you play guitar and are a good mechanic? That's great! I can use that too." But in order for God to use them, we must throw them down at His feet and relinquish control of them to Him. Only then can God work through them. It's difficult and scary to fully surrender what you have to the Lord. That's why we tend to keep taking it back. So how do you know when you have truly released control? Only when you can willingly accept whatever happens to it, is it truly out of your grasp. Only then have we completely given it to God.

When Moses surrendered his staff, he didn't know what would happen next. What happened was definitely not what he expected. Perhaps he thought God would bless the staff and he would become a more prosperous shepherd. But the staff turned into a poisonous snake, which alarmed Moses and he ran from it. That is why it is so hard for us to give up control. We don't know what will happen. Deep down we suspect that God's plan and agenda might be different from ours. We want God to make our life safe and comfortable but He wants to make us overcoming sons and daughters. God told Moses to, "*Stretch out your hand and grasp it by the tail.*" That is probably the last thing that Moses wanted to do, after all, he had just run from it. Moses felt afraid of the snake but his trust in God was greater than his fear so he picked up the snake. Is there something you don't want to face but God is telling you to go to it and pick it up? Perhaps it is a past hurt or failure that God wants you to face and overcome by His power. Perhaps it is some great challenge that lies before you. It may be something scary, but will you be like Moses and choose to let your trust in God be greater than your fear?

When Moses picked up the serpent, it became his shepherd's staff once again. But now it was charged with God's power. He would one day use that staff to part the Red Sea. All his skills and knowledge were greatly multiplied through God. Picking up the snake did not destroy him, it enlarged him. He threw down a staff that tended sheep but picked up one that would shepherd Israel. When you are willing to surrender your "little" to God, it becomes "much." When you are willing to face you fears rather than run from them, you become an overcomer. Fear robs us of God's calling and blessing but faith makes us God's mighty people. Will you surrender control and trust God today?

Prayer - Lord I want to be fruitful for You. I want to be an overcomer. Help me to realize the potential of what I already have when I release ownership and control to You. I choose to trust in Your goodness and faithfulness rather than cling to my own plans. Help me to be like Moses, that my trust in God would be greater than my fear of the unknown.

Your Home Is an Embassy

"Now all these things are from God, who reconciled us to Himself through Christ and gave us the ministry of reconciliation, namely, that God was in Christ reconciling the world to Himself, not counting their trespasses against them, and He has committed to us the word of reconciliation. Therefore, we are ambassadors for Christ, as though God were making an appeal through us; we beg you on behalf of Christ, be reconciled to God." II Corinthians 5:18-20

Jesus Christ was Heaven's ambassador sent to earth. His mission was to reconcile us to God. He did this through His teaching and His death on the cross. The need to reconcile means there's been a breach, a broken relationship, and resulting alienation. People are alienated from God. They hide from Him, they distrust Him, and they resist His rule.

When people are alienated from God, it leads to being alienated from each other – from spouses, family members, people of other races, etc. Much of the present conflict and alienation in our society is rooted in our alienation from God. But when people are reconciled to God, they can then be reconciled to each other. When Jesus' mission was complete, Heaven recalled its ambassador back home. Before leaving, He entrusted to us the ministry of reconciling people to God. Even more, He passed on the role of ambassador to each of us. We read in the passage above, *"Therefore we are ambassadors for Christ..."* We speak for Him, carry His commission and conduct His affairs.

Reflect on what it means to be an ambassador. Every ambassador serves in a foreign country but represents the interests of their home country where they are a citizen. We read, in Philippians 3:20, that *"our citizenship is in Heaven."* Every day we are to represent the interests of Heaven. Also, an ambassador, though far from home, carries his government's full authority. Likewise, Jesus has given us full authority. Our job is to bring Heaven's riches to meet the needs around us.

Remember that an ambassador doesn't look to his own interests first, but to those of his country that sent him. Neither does an ambassador get to choose where he or she is posted. I'm sure that most ambassadors would choose the more desirable postings like England or Sweden, but America also has interests in Iraq and Sudan that need to be taken care of. Often, the less desirable locations prove to be the most important. Sometimes, as Christians, we complain about our job, the neighborhood we live in, or the politics of those who run our city or state. Instead, we should accept these things as the Lord's assignment until He moves us. Jesus assigns His ambassadors where He needs them.

You can be faithful and productive wherever you are posted, no matter how difficult it is. Instead of listing everything wrong with your assignment, ask yourself, "What would this place be like if the Lord had not sent me here?" If you are truly being salt and light, you have already made it better. Try to see each person as Christ sees them. Learn to see every need or problem as an opportunity for God to demonstrate His love, faithfulness, and power through you.

The Apostle Paul, while in prison in Ephesus, said of himself, *"I am an ambassador in chains"* (Eph. 6:20). Although he had been thrown in jail, he accepted it as his next assignment to represent Jesus. Besides his ministry to the guards and other prisoners, Paul wrote four of his New Testament epistles during this period. They are known as the prison epistles. Because he was willing to accept his posting and serve as an ambassador, countless believers down through the ages have been blessed.

Many years ago, I realized that if I am an ambassador, then my home is an embassy. When Jesus was born, God only had one embassy on earth. It was the temple in Jerusalem. People had to go there to offer sacrifices, celebrate the Old Testament feasts, and gather during national crises to pray to God. But God had a plan to put an embassy in every neighborhood. If you are an ambassador, then your home is an embassy of the Kingdom of God. A neighborhood embassy should lift up prayer for that neighborhood and all the needs in it. It should demonstrate the culture of Heaven, proclaim Heaven's message, offer refuge, and enroll new citizens.

Wherever a person works, there is likely at least one ambassador there, and wherever they live there is an embassy close by. If I am an ambassador and my home an embassy, then I must reach out to coworkers and neighbors. I can prayer-walk the neighborhood, greet everyone who walks by, bring gifts to my neighbors, and invite them over. God has called and commissioned us as ambassadors of Heaven. There is no higher or greater position imaginable.

Prayer – Thank You for the high honor of making me an ambassador and my home an embassy. Help me to be a faithful and effective representative of my King. Help me to fulfill my duties by the power and authority of the Kingdom of God.

Day 56

The Jar and the Stone

"While He was in Bethany at the home of Simon the leper, and reclining at the table, there came a woman with an alabaster vial of very costly perfume of pure nard; and she broke the vial and poured it over His head." Mark 14:3

The costly perfume the women poured over Jesus' head is identified as "pure nard" which was produced from a root native to India. It was perhaps the most expensive of perfumes. It was sealed up in a beautiful long-necked vial of alabaster to preserve its aroma. The vial itself was beautiful but its long neck had to be broken to release the perfume. The treasure was not the vial but what was in the vial.

In the same way, Paul writes in II Corinthians 4:7, *"But we have this treasure in earthen vessels, so that the surpassing greatness of the power will be of God and not of ourselves."* The treasure Paul is speaking of is identified in the previous verse as *"the glory of God"* (II Cor. 4:6). Paul refers to us as common earthen storage jars that contain God's glory and power. The glory is not the clay vessels but rather in what they contain. In order for the world to see that glory, the outward clay vessel must be broken. This is God's plan but we resist it because we love our outward clay vessel. We all want God's glory to be released but we often draw back from the cost of giving up our will, plans, pride and self-love. But breaking the clay vessel is the price of releasing God's glory and life.

God has a plan to help us overcome this dilemma. I Peter 2:6 quotes from several Old Testament passages and reads, " *BEHOLD I LAY IN ZION A CHOICE STONE, A PRECIOUS CORNER STONE, AND HE WHO BELIEVES IN HIM WILL NOT BE DISAPPOINTED.' This precious value is for you who believe; but for those who disbelieve, 'THE STONE WHICH THE BUILDERS REJECTED, THIS BECAME THE VERY CORNER STONE', 'AND A STONE OF STUMBLING AND A ROCK OF OFFENSE.'* " It is just one stone, but it is, at the same time, both a cornerstone and a stone of stumbling. It is a stone of stumbling to rebellion and unbelief but a cornerstone to the one who believes and obeys. What is this stone? The stone is Jesus and it requires humbling yourself before Him. The religious leaders of Jesus' time had prayed and waited their entire life for God to deliver them and set up His Kingdom but when God visited them in the person of Jesus, they saw Him as a *"Rock of Offense"* and they rejected Him. They were offended by, and couldn't accept, this outsider who threatened their power, status and plans. Paul wrote that the Jewish leaders stumbled over the stumbling stone (Rom. 9:32). But for those who accepted Him, He became the foundation stone for a new life of salvation and restoration.

The Stumbling Stone is a spiritual life principal. It's not just about our initial salvation. It is present in all of our transactions with God. Before we can experience a spiritual breakthrough or growth and victory, we must embrace a stumbling - a rock of offense. Whenever we encounter one, everything within us that can disqualify us from God's victory (such as pride, doubt and self-centeredness), rises up to resist and turn us away. The purpose of a stumbling stone is to break our clay vessel so that we will release and experience the supernatural. Jesus said of the stumbling stone, *"And he who falls on this stone will be broken to pieces; but on whomever it falls, it will scatter him like dust"* (Matt. 21:44). Jesus is saying, if we embrace the rock of offense and fall on it, our pride, self-will and fear will be broken and the inner treasure released (but, if instead, we turn away, we will be crushed under the judgement of sin). The natural must be broken so the supernatural can be released. The natural is what you are capable of in yourself, limited by all your pride, weakness and ignorance. The supernatural is above and beyond the natural. It is what God can do in and through you. Self-centered love must be broken so that we can experience and express Christ's love. Boastful self-sufficiency must be broken before we are candidates to receive the fullness of Christ's supply and help.

A stumbling stone can come to us in many forms. Christ's command to forgive someone, or to admit we were wrong and apologize, or to willingly submit to an imperfect leader, or to move to a certain neighborhood can all be rocks of offense that we draw back from. But, we can only become who Christ wants us to be and receive what He wants to give us by facing them. You cannot go around them; you must go through them. My brother, Dave, says that finally being willing to submit to and serve a very imperfect and difficult leader was the key to God releasing him to a new and powerful ministry. Take a moment and consider this question: *"What blessing or goal do I seek?"* And then ask yourself, *"What stumbling stone might God have placed between me and that blessing?"*

Prayer - I proclaim that You are the Treasure and Glory of my life. Give me the understanding to recognize the stumbling stones You have place before me, and the courage to embrace them. May Your life-giving aroma be released through my life.

What Are You Waiting For?

"But do not let this one fact escape your notice, beloved, that with the Lord one day is like a thousand years, and a thousand years like one day. The Lord is not slow about His promise, as some count slowness, but is patient toward you, not wishing for any to perish but for all to come to repentance." II Peter 3:8-9

Many of you are like me. I don't like to be kept waiting. Yet most of the best things in my life required that I wait for them. They didn't come easily or quickly, although I wished that they would. I have learned that God doesn't seem to care about my timetable or my impatience. Therefore, I have had to learn how to wait. Waiting on God is a fact of life for each of us.

Today's passage teaches us several important facts. First, it teaches us that God does not view time the way we do. He has a different perspective, and we have to be able to rest in His superior knowledge and wisdom. The second thing we learn is that God is not slow or late in His actions. Rather, He is patient. He waits until people and events line up to allow His perfect result. God always acts with purpose. He never does the wrong thing, nor does He ever act at the wrong time. Many times in the past, I wondered why God was keeping me waiting. Years later, I would look back and realize that I hadn't been waiting on God – rather, He had been waiting on me. I wasn't ready for what I wanted. God had been patiently preparing me until I was ready.

The Bible often compares our growth and enlargement to a farmer sowing seed and reaping a harvest. Between sowing the seed and gaining the harvest is a growing season. The farmer would, no doubt, like the harvest to come immediately. It is the same with us. Between our request and its fulfilment there is often a growing season, a process in which we grow. It is going through that process that matures and prepares us. For a tree to become great, it must not only grow high, but it must also grow down deep. It sends its roots down deep during dry seasons searching for water. In the same way, waiting on God develops depth in us.

God has a different view of waiting than we do. We see waiting as an inconvenience. God sees it as a process of transformation. Our human nature tends to seek God's gifts even more than we seek the Giver of those gifts. We want health, prosperity, happiness and a solution to all our problems. As long as these come to us easily and quickly, we have a tendency to take God for granted. We don't hunger for Him much or develop a deep faith. But when our answers don't come quickly, we turn our attention to God in prayer, search the Bible for answers and search our hearts for hindrances. We ask God to speak to us and give us understanding. In other words, in waiting for the gifts, we learn to wait upon the Giver. And as we do, we are transformed more into His image and gain strength and understanding. In my life, my greatest spiritual growth came from waiting on God for something I needed. We start out seeking God for some gift, but in the waiting process we gain knowledge and greater friendship with God.

Waiting on God actually empowers us. Isaiah 40:31 states, "Yet those who wait for the Lord will gain new strength; they will mount up with wings like eagles, they will run and not get tired." As we wait and learn to trust in God, we gain a new kind of strength, a supernatural strength. And if we wait, we will also see the great works of God. Isaiah 64:4 tells us that God *"acts in behalf of the one who waits for Him."* To wait on God means to focus your love and attention on Him, and to continue to believe and be thankful despite delays and seeming setbacks.

Prayer – God, help me to be content to wait upon Your timing, trusting in Your wisdom. Help me to find the great benefit that comes from waiting upon You. Help me to learn to seek Your face more than I seek the gifts from Your hand. Help me to gain new strength and wisdom in this season.

How God Reveals Himself

*"The heavens are telling of the glory of God; And their expanse
is declaring the works of His hands." Psalm 19:1*

(Please read entire Psalm 19 for this devotion)

Psalm 19 is a celebration of God's revelation to us. Aren't you glad
God is not hiding from us, nor is He silent. He wants us to know
Him and His kind purposes for us. This psalm celebrates that fact.
This psalm divides into three parts - each one dealing with a
different avenue God uses to reveal Himself to us. The first 6
verses talk about general or natural revelation in which God
reveals Himself through what He has made. Our psalm begins with
King David peering up into the heavens in awe and declaring, *"The
heavens are telling of the glory of God.... day to day pours forth
speech, and night to night reveals knowledge"* (Ps. 19: 1, 2). If you
have ever been out in the desert or mountains on a clear night, it
is awe inspiring; it takes your breath away. Nature appears even
more wondrous when seen through a powerful electron
microscope or a great telescope in a space observatory. It tells us
of God's wisdom and grandeur.

Now general revelation is enough to tell us there is a God and
something about His character and nature, but it can only take us
so far. Since God wants us to know Him, He's given us Scripture as
a second avenue to communicate with us. We read of it in verses

7-11. Now in the first section (vs. 1-6) the generic Hebrew name for God is used "*El.*" But the second section (vs. 7-11) is a higher form of revelation, giving us deeper knowledge of God, so a different name for God is used, the name, "*Yahweh.*" This is God's personal or covenant name. To know God by this name requires more than what we can learn through nature. It requires God's self-revelation in words. This is known as *Special Revelation.* In the Bible, God personally reveals Himself to us and gives to us His covenant promises. Psalm 19:7-11 outlines some of the blessings Scripture holds for us. Through God's promises and commandments, He can restore a human soul no matter how broken, teach us the wisdom to succeed, put joy in our heart and light up our eyes. They can direct our steps into great blessing and guard us from danger. What a great gift the Bible is! How can we ever measure its value? Of course, it does us little good unless we read and study it.

Now, God has made a third avenue of revelation available to us. For God has not only inspired the Scriptures, but He puts His Spirit in us to guide us, encourage us and convince us of His Truth. This third avenue is the *illumination of the Holy Spirit*. In this third section of Psalm 19, we learn of the wonderful work of the Holy Spirit. He illuminates even the most hidden parts of our heart, revealing error and showing us truth (v.12). He empowers us to overcome sin rather than be mastered by it (v.13). He works within us to transform our heart to become more pleasing to God (v.14). The Holy Spirit can give us visions and dreams and inspire our imagination and meditations. At times He will inspire the words of others to speak to us through prophecy. How wonderful it is to have the Holy Spirit as our Counselor, Guide and Comforter.

Remember, God is not hiding from us, nor is He silent. He is actively communicating to us if only we will see and hear. May the words of Jesus be true of you, *"But blessed be your eyes because they see, and your ears because they hear"* (Matt. 13:16).

Prayer - Help me to open up my spiritual eyes and ears so You can speak to me. Help me to treasure the Bible and the gift of Your Spirit. Let the words of my mouth and the meditations of my heart be acceptable in Your sight.

True Knowledge

"Knowledge makes arrogant, but love edifies. If anyone supposes that he knows anything, he has not yet known as he ought to know, but if anyone loves God, he is known by Him."
I Corinthians 8:1-3

Did you know there was a right way of knowing things and also a wrong way of knowing things? The one who has wrong knowledge, "... *has not yet known as he ought to know.*" We read that such wrong knowledge leads to arrogance (and arrogance leads to division, conflict, and a lack of love). But verse 3 points us to a higher way of knowing which is through fellowship with God.

What is the wrong way of knowing? It is trying to understand life apart from God, the influence of the Holy Spirit and the truth of His Word. When we interpret facts and events by our limited understanding, narrow self-interest and sinful desires, it always results in error, division, envy, unhappiness and anxiety. Fear, conflict and suffering entered our world when, under Satan's influence, Adam and Eve chose to pursue knowledge and understanding apart from God. They chose to eat from the Tree of the Knowledge of Good and Evil rather than the Tree of Life (Gen. 3:4-7).

To eat from that tree represents the attempt to understand yourself and all of life apart from God and His Truth. It is trying to find truth by yourself rather than through God. What was the result of Adam and Eve's choice? They realized they were naked and unprotected. Fear and shame entered their heart. They became divided, and Adam blamed Eve. This is where eating from that tree always leads. It can't give you what the Tree of Life can.

Verse 2 of our passage represents the Tree of Knowledge. But verse 3 points us to the Tree of Life which is rooted in love and leads to right knowledge. In Philippians 1:9-10, Paul writes, "*And this I pray, that your love may abound still more and more in real knowledge and all discernment, so that you may approve the things that are excellent...*" True knowledge is rooted in love. True knowledge begins with being secure in knowing God loves you and then loving Him in return. I only became truly free to recognize and accept the truth when I was no longer afraid or insecure. Unless I am motivated by love, I will become a self-seeking truth twister, because I will be driven by fear, pride, or selfish desire. The only way to gain true knowledge is through love. It doesn't come through education and study alone.

True knowledge comes when I seek God and His Word in order to understand. Everything can either be rightly seen and perceived in God's Light, or it will be misinterpreted and misunderstood in the absence of that light. All things are only seen clearly in His Light. The pursuit of knowledge outside of God's Light leads to foolishness and despair. This is why our universities are so full of confusion, division and alienation.

Pursuing the knowledge of God and His love is the greatest thing. It's of far greater profit than pursuing the knowledge of ourselves. For only when we know God will we understand ourselves. Only God can truly show us our purpose. *The great issue in life is not **who** you are. The great issue is **whose** you are.* That is,

Who made you? Who redeemed you? Who loves you? Who goes before you? and Who empowers you? Resting in that knowledge allows you to eat from the Tree of Life every day. It is the great secret of life. Every day we decide which tree to eat from. One leads to love, joy and true knowledge; the other to arrogance, division, fear and hatred.

Prayer - I desire to see and know all things in Your light. I will seek You and Your Word in order that I might truly understand myself and all things. Help me to pursue Your knowledge above anything else. I believe it is the highest and most important thing.

Made in the USA
Monee, IL
28 October 2022

16659813R00121